D0160497

THE DEAN OF AMERICAN LETTERS

The Late Career of
WILLIAM DEAN HOWELLS

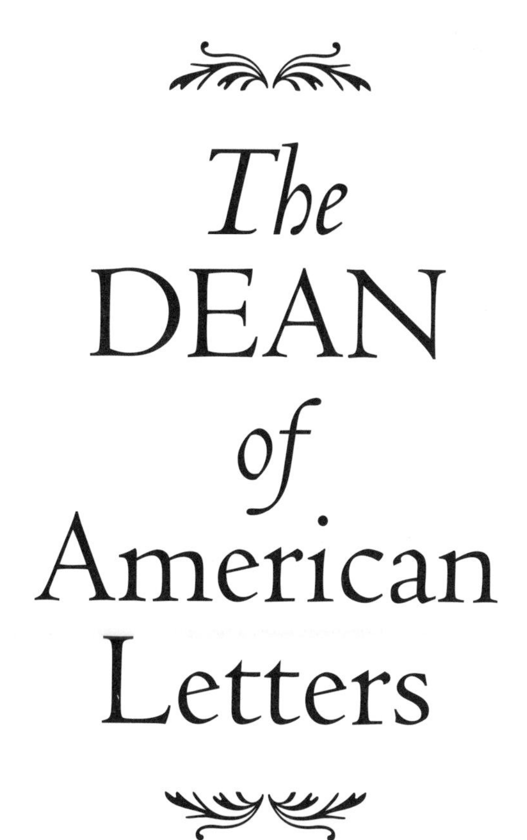

The DEAN *of* American Letters

John W. Crowley

UNIVERSITY OF MASSACHUSETTS PRESS
Amherst

Printed in the United States of America
LC 99-29050
ISBN 1-55849-240-2
Designed by Milenda Nan Ok Lee
Printed and bound by Sheridan Books, Inc.

Library of Congress Cataloging-in-Publication Data
Crowley, John William, 1945–
The Dean of American Letters : the late career of William Dean
Howells / John W. Crowley.
p. cm.
Includes bibliographical references and index.
ISBN 1-55849-240-2 (cloth : alk. paper)
1. Howells, William Dean, 1837–1920—Last years. 2. Novelists,
American—19th century Biography. 3. Critics—United States
Biography. I. Title.
PS2033.C74 1999
813′.4—dc21
[B]
99-29050
CIP

British Library Cataloguing in Publication data are available.

In memory of my father,

John A. Crowley Jr.

and

in tribute to the men

who mentored me,

especially

Edwin E. Barlow

CONTENTS

ACKNOWLEDGMENTS

I am grateful to David J. Nordloh for helpful suggestions. For permission to reuse material first published elsewhere, I thank *The New England Quarterly,* in which part of chapter 5 first appeared, and the University of Missouri Press, publisher of *Biographies of Books: The Compositional Histories of Notable American Writings* (1996), edited by James Barbour and Tom Quirk, in which part of chapter 1 first appeared.

THE DEAN OF AMERICAN LETTERS

INTRODUCTION

Bill of Particulars

A FEW YEARS AGO, during a brief vogue of mistress memoirs (boudoir tittle-tattle of the wannabe rich and famous), Veronica Geng reluctantly disclosed her torrid affair with Chairman Mao:

> Until now, writing a book about this well-known man has been the farthest thing from my mind—except perhaps for writing a book about someone else. . . . But how can I hide while other women publish? Even my friends are at it. Betty Ann is writing *Konnie!: Adenauer in Love.* Cathy and Joan are collaborating on *Yalta Groupies.* And my Great-Aunt Harriet has just received a six-figure advance for *"Bill" of Particulars: An Intimate Memoir of William Dean Howells.*

Geng later divulges that "Bill" lavished on Harriet some characteristically tasteful baubles: "a diamond brooch in the form of five ribbon loops terminating in diamond-set tassels, and an aquamarine-and-diamond tiara with scroll and quill-pen motifs separated by single oblong-cut stones mounted on an aquamarine-and-diamond band."[1]

The cream of this jest, of course, is the impossibility of believing that William Dean Howells would ever have taken a lover: that this icon of Victorian probity, starched in the shirt of his triple-barreled name, could ever have unbuttoned into just plain (and randy!) "Bill." Given Howells's twentieth-century reputation as an archprude, fixated on the smiling (but blind to the leering) aspects of life, it's hard enough to believe—evidence of his recurrent paternity notwithstanding—that he had any sex life at all. He could not imaginably have written about it; while he was roundly abused for his defense of Zola, Ibsen, and other purveyors of foreign "smut," Howells never wavered from his own commitment to decent homespun values. *His* work, he once indignantly insisted to Richard Watson Gilder, "would be always suitable to a family magazine."[2]

The context for this remark was a negotiation in 1893 about selling some stories to the *Century,* over which Gilder's editorial will-to-power was expressed in a plan to build "some small loop-hole" into all contracts, even with established writers, so that he would never be bound in advance to accept any given submission. In asking Howells for such an understanding, Gilder explained: "We hit upon a phrase with a very celebrated author, lately. It was merely, I think, that the story should be always suitable to a family magazine. . . . I suppose some such knot-hole as that would not discommode you, and would 'keep our record clear' " (*SL,* 4:42 n).

Howells was not merely discommoded; he was furious that Gilder would think to engage a story from him "with any sort of misgiving in your mind." He demanded none other than the terms he had always enjoyed: outright and unconditional acceptance from the start. Here, he huffed, was "a loophole as large as all outdoors, wide open to you" (*SL,* 4:45). Gilder must have jumped through it, for no Howells contribution appeared in the *Century* for two years.

In 1893, at the peak of his imaginative powers, Howells had so much clout in the literary marketplace that he could well afford to stare down any editor. As Edwin H. Cady observes, "Nobody knew the business of authorship better than Howells." With his long and varied experience and his knack for shrewd dealing, he "had discovered, certainly like no one before, and possibly like no one after, how to make writing pay steadily, fully, even handsomely without selling out either his artistic or civic conscience. In this, too, he was the nation's leading author."[3]

In 1893, however, America's leading author had not yet become The Dean of American Letters, the exalted role into which Howells was involuntarily cast by a grateful nation, the status that proved ultimately disastrous for his literary reputation. On the contrary, well into the 1890s, Howells still retained a reputation for (1) unruly polemics, as a consequence of his acerbic campaign against neoromanticism in *Harper's* "Editor's Study," and (2) unsound politics, as a result of his public plea for the executed Chicago anarchists in 1887 and his identification with socialist causes.

Dubbed a "parlor anarchist" by his old friend, Whitelaw Reid, the putatively pugnacious Howells was anathema in some quarters: for instance, to the sleek and leisured editors of *Life,* the highbrow humor magazine that regularly renounced "Mr. Trowells" and all his works: "Chief among them are 'A Chance Acquaintance; or, Miss Middleton's Lover'; 'Their Wedding Journey; or, Parted on their Bridal Tour'; 'Dr. Breen's Practice; or, the Morphine Habit's Victim'; 'A Foregone Conclusion; or, the Straight Tip on the Suburban'; and 'Indian Summer; or, the Quick or the Dead.' "[4]

By the last two decades of Howells's life, however, his public image had undergone a sea change. Not only was he no longer controversial; he was now perceived as unexceptionable, a kind of living monument, a national treasure beloved by all except, perhaps, a few brash young writers with chips on their shoulders and no due respect for their elders. In 1910, William Lyon Phelps, the popular Yale professor, defended Howells from the sneers of Gertrude Atherton and others evidently averse to "his intense ethical earnestness." Phelps argued that Howells's distinctive style—"that quiet stingless humor, clever dialogue, and wholesome charm"—had become synonymous with the author himself, what readers naturally associated with his name. Thus the work is "a clear manifestation of his own personality"; while critics may differ about the "permanent value and final place" of the work, Howells's personality is

> one that irresistibly commands our highest respect and our warmest affection. A simple, democratic, unaffected, modest, kindly, humorous, healthy soul, with a rare combination of rugged virility and extreme refinement. It is exceedingly fortunate for America that such a man has for so many years by common consent, at home and abroad, been regarded as the Dean of American Letters. He has had more influence on the output of fiction in America than any other living man. This influence has been entirely wholesome, from the standpoint of both morals and Art.[5]

This portrait of Howells is recognizable as the prim and proper Dean so hilariously at odds with Aunt Harriet's "Bill" of particulars.

How did Howells become The Dean? Cady explains that as his preeminence became "increasingly a matter of fact," the inviting pun on his middle name became "increasingly irresistible." No one thought to take credit for the coinage: "It just drifted into casual use" (p. 223). In the following chapters, I account more precisely for W. D. Howells's transformation into William Dean Howells, The Dean of American Letters. My objective in tracing the development of Howells's career after 1890 is to show his implication in the modern business of authorship that was rapidly evolving during the same period. The monumentalized Dean was, I believe, an early manifestation of the commodification of the literary marketplace that has governed American letters throughout the twentieth century.

Let me be clear about the genre of this book. Along with *The Black Heart's Truth* (1985) and *The Mask of Fiction* (1989), *The Dean of American Letters* constitutes a trilogy that covers Howells's life and work from one end to the other. But whereas *The Black Heart's Truth* and *The Mask of Fiction* explored Howells's interiority as a writer, *The Dean* treats his public career as a literary personage. I do not, however, offer a comprehensive survey of the literary marketplace within which Howells operated. That would repeat several existing studies on American cultural literacy, the construction of authorship, and the history of the publishing industry. My emphasis falls less on Howells's actual status in the literary trade than on his *perception* of shifting actualities in the business of authorship and his strategic responses to those changes. In other words, at the interface of Howells with the marketplace, I am attuned to Howells's own point of view, even when his apprehensions may have differed from objective facts about his literary position.

This book, then, resembles its two predecessors in being a kind of life writing.

But none of the volumes in my Howells trilogy, nor the three together, qualifies as a proper biography in the traditional sense of a coherent and continuous narrative of a subject's life story. *The Dean of American Letters* progresses chronologically but very selectively. I make no attempt to flesh out the last thirty years of W. D. Howells (as opposed to William Dean Howells), although such a detailed account would be a welcome supplement to Edwin H. Cady's magisterial *The Realist at War* (1958).[6]

In this study, it matters less who or what Howells "really" was than what he was made to seem and to represent. I am concerned primarily with the manufacture of his symbolic cultural role; once "Howells" had been commodified, he became most "real" as the unreal Dean of American Letters. All the while, his vestigial "self" (whatever identity he carried over from his Victorian youth) had uneasily to coexist with this strange new creature of modern publicity.

The Dean of American Letters thus focuses rather narrowly (also sharply, I hope) on The Dean's special cultural authority and the vicissitudes of his literary reputation. Beginning at the height of Howells's career in 1890, I trace his creative decline and, at the same time, his ascension to glory as an exemplar of the American Victorian ethos. The final chapter explores the demolition of The Dean during the teens and twenties. What animates *The Dean of American Letters*—and what binds my Howells trilogy together—is an enduring curiosity about the intersection of Howells's ordinary and imaginative lives: the same conjunction that defined Howellsian realism itself.

I

HOWELLS IN 1890

The Unsmiling Aspects of Life

SOON AFTER he took over *Harper's* "Editor's Study" in 1886, W. D. Howells "rather absently dynamited his own reputation for the next century."[1] Writing of *Crime and Punishment,* which he had recently read in a French translation, Howells related the "hardly less tragical story" of Dostoevsky's own life: how he was marched before the firing squad and then reprieved at the last second—only to be sentenced to six years' hard labor in Siberia. "Whatever their deserts," Howells added sardonically,

> very few American novelists have been led out to be shot, or finally exiled to the rigors of a winter at Duluth; one might make Herr Most the hero of a labor-question romance with perfect impunity; and in a land where journeymen carpenters and plumbers strike for four dollars a day the sum of hunger and cold is certainly very small, and the wrong from class to class is almost inappreciable. We invite our novelists, therefore, to concern themselves with the more smiling aspects of life, which are the more American, and to seek the universal in the individual rather than the social interests.

Howells was undoubtedly correct that life in the United States was less arduous, *on average,* than life in Russia. Appropriately, then, an American realist committed to the representation of ordinary experience—an indigenous reality of the commonplace, defined in part by contrast to such reality elsewhere—should concern himself, as a Dostoevsky could not, with the relatively "more smiling aspects" of life. Precisely because "there were so few shadows and inequalities in our broad level of prosperity," the native realist could not honestly write an American *Crime and Punishment:* "whoever struck a note so profoundly tragic in American fiction would do a false and mistaken thing."[2]

Although the logic here is impeccable *if* one accepts both Howells's theory of realism and his undergirding premise about American prosperity, some readers over the last century have gagged on the "smiling aspects of life" and pilloried

Howells for his supposed complacency about "the social interests"—seen as an unforgivable blindness to the less smiling aspects of the Gilded Age.

By 1889, in the midst of writing *A Hazard of New Fortunes,* Howells himself seemed to know better. As he confessed to Edmund Gosse, a friend privy to his inmost thoughts, his mood had now darkened considerably: "No, black care has not left so much laugh in me as there used to be" (*SL,* 3:245). And when he later incorporated the notorious "Editor's Study" into *Criticism and Fiction* (1891), Howells subtly revised it: "and the wrong from class to class *has been* almost inappreciable, *though all this is changing for the worse*" (my emphasis).[3]

He also deleted the clause about Herr Most and the labor-question romance.

I

JOHANN MOST set forth from London in 1882 to carry the gospel of European anarchism to the new world. Preaching violent resistance to the capitalist regime, Most published a handbook on revolution in which he proffered the recipes for dynamite and other high explosives.

Few Americans perceived much difference among the various "foreign" doctrines—anarchism, socialism, communism—that were suspected of breeding discontent throughout the 1880s, a tumultuous decade of unprecedented strife between Labor and Capital. Whatever the political principles espoused by workers, however modest or reasonable their goals, all "agitation" was "connected in the public mind with attacks upon the dearest beliefs of Americans: religion, freedom, and prosperity."[4]

Early in 1886, in one of many such conflicts across the United States, workers subjected to a general lockout picketed the McCormick Reaper Works in Chicago. On 3 May, about the time Howells was endorsing the "smiling aspects,"[5] a clash between strikers and their scab replacements triggered police intervention; several workers were beaten and shot, at least two of them fatally. The following evening a protest in Haymarket Square was attended by the mayor of Chicago as well as labor organizers and political radicals. The rally was rhetorically supercharged but uneventful until the end—after the mayor had departed—when the police unnecessarily moved to disperse the already diminishing crowd and a bomb exploded, killing one policeman, mortally wounding six others (all of whom died within a few weeks), and injuring dozens more. As the enraged police fired into the fleeing crowd, many of the workers also were wounded.

The bomb-thrower's identity was never determined, but the police nevertheless rounded up eight prominent anarchists—George Engel, Samuel Fielden, Adolph Fischer, Louis Lingg, Oscar Neebe, Albert Parsons, Michael Schwab, and August Spies—and charged them with the murder of Officer Mathias J. Degan. In effect, the accused were indicted for their incendiary political beliefs. Whether they had been present at the Haymarket rally or not (most of them had, in fact, been elsewhere when the bomb went off), the anarchists were held strictly accountable for inciting the violence. Promptly brought to trial, all were convicted on 20 August 1886. In October, the presiding judge denied a defense motion for a new trial and condemned seven of them to hang. The executions were stayed, however, while lawyers appealed to higher courts. Meanwhile, a vindictive national mood, fomented by the press, magnified the anarchists' case into a symbol, not of any "wrong from class to class," but rather of the perceived peril to basic American values.

A year later, just before the prisoners' appeal was denied by the Illinois Supreme Court, Howells explained that his "original feeling that the trial of the anarchists was hysterical and unjust" had been strengthened by his reading an account that one of their partisans had sent him anonymously.[6] "I feel that these men are doomed to suffer for their opinions' sake," he told George W. Curtis, editorial writer for *Harper's Weekly;* "the trial was for socialism and not for murder." The case had taken "deep hold" of the novelist: "I feel strongly the calamity which error in it must embody. Civilization cannot afford to give martyrs to a bad cause; and if the cause of these men is good, what an awful mistake to put them to death!" (*SL*, 3:193).

Although Howells was very well aware that *Harper's Weekly* had allied itself editorially with the vast majority in demanding retribution, he hoped that Curtis, whose record of social activism Howells had long admired, might still be persuaded to speak out. There was time, perhaps, to temper public fury before the United States Supreme Court rendered its final judgment. But Curtis, an erstwhile abolitionist, retreated from his earlier, privately confessed doubts of the anarchists' guilt, pleading that he was too ignorant of the trial to take a position on its fairness. He urged Howells to pursue the matter himself: "Now your name would give great weight to any statement or plea proceeding evidently not from emotion, but from conviction." Yes, *Harper's Weekly* might print such a plea, but it "would have to be very conclusive, undoubtedly, to strike our friends in Franklin Square favorably."[7]

Howells's friends in Franklin Square were the publishers who had recently signed him to an exclusive contract. Following the failure of James R. Osgood and Company in Boston, Howells, who had been a freelancer since resigning his editorship of the *Atlantic Monthly* in 1881, came to lucrative terms with Harper and Brothers in October 1885. For a salary of $10,000, he agreed to produce one novel yearly for serial and book publication, as well as one farce and other material for *Harper's Monthly* and *Harper's Weekly*—for all of which work he would also receive generous royalties (12.5 percent) and piecework payments. For an additional $3,000, he would write the "Editor's Study," beginning in January 1886. Other than Howells's letters, in fact, the Harpers owned the rights to everything he wrote.[8]

Thus when it became clear that Curtis would not budge, Howells decided to make his views public through a letter to the *New York Tribune.* The question of justice or injustice, he sternly prophesied, "must remain for history, which judges the judgment of courts . . . and I, for one, cannot doubt what the decision of history will be" (*SL,* 3:199). Howells's appeal appeared just five days before Engel, Fischer, Parsons, and Spies went to the gallows on 11 November 1887. Lingg had committed suicide on the eve of his execution; the other two anarchists had been spared the death penalty.

Among prominent literary figures, Howells was not merely "for one" in decrying the hangings; he was alone. He had implored John Greenleaf Whittier, for instance, to appeal for clemency from the governor of Illinois: "A letter from you would have great weight with him. I beseech you to write it, and do what one great and blameless man may to avert the cruellest wrong that ever threatened our fame as a nation" (*SL,* 3:198). But a man who, like Curtis, had once defied authority in the cause of abolition proved to be timorous now, washing his hands of the anarchists on the punctilious grounds that he had "never interfered with the law as it affects individual cases" (*SL,* 3:199 n).[9] Isolated in an extremely unpopular stand, Howells became a lightning rod for the shafts of those who cheered the hangings he denounced as "the thing forever damnable before God and abominable to civilized men" (*SL,* 3:200).

A day later, in a second letter to the *Tribune,* Howells apologized with fierce sarcasm for intruding "a note of regret" upon the "hymn of thanksgiving for blood going up from thousands of newspapers all over the land this morning." He insisted that the hangings had been nothing other than a "political execution": "*They died, in the prime of the freest Republic the world has ever known, for their opinions' sake.*" At great length he excoriated those responsible, in their "paroxysmal righteousness," for "a trial by passion, by terror, by prejudice, by hate, by newspaper." Intending, perhaps, to shame Curtis and Whittier, Howells invoked the spirits of Emerson, Garrison, Parker, Phillips, Thoreau, and others who had dared to fight against slavery—all of whom, by the contorted logic of the anarchists' trial, should also have merited death for inciting the violence of John Brown. "I dread the Anarchy of the Courts," he defiantly concluded, "but I have never been afraid of the prevalence of the dead Anarchists' doctrine, because that must always remain to plain common sense, unthinkable; and I am not afraid of any acts of revenge from their fellow conspirators because I believe they never were part of any conspiracy" (*SL,* 3:201–4).

This letter, titled "A Word for the Dead," was evidently never sent. A draft addressed to Whitelaw Reid, editor of the *Tribune,* was found among Howells's papers by Edwin H. Cady and first published by him in 1958. It seems more likely that Howells never mailed the letter than that Reid received but refused to publish it. Cady believes that once Howells had vented his wrath in the writing of "A Word for the Dead," he thought better of exposing himself to "unfair but even more withering attack from a press and public opinion already passionately decided. It had destroyed the Anarchists and it might destroy him."[10]

The same day, 12 November 1887, that Howells banked the fire of his indignation, Johann Most was arrested for delivering an inflammatory speech in protest of the executions. Most's subsequent incarceration struck Howells as yet another injustice: "This can't last. Sometime the conscience of the people will be stirred" (*SL*, 3:210).

Howells's own conscience had already been stirred, more deeply than he would have thought possible a few years earlier. But his reaction to the Haymarket affair was far more circumspect than Johann Most's. In demanding justice for the anarchists, Howells never committed himself to their cause. Although he believed that August Spies was "a noble, unselfish and heroic soul," he also had his "reservations in regard to him" (*SL*, 3:209), and he distanced himself from those who touted Spies as a revolutionary martyr. "How hard it is," he reflected, "when a great wrong has been done, not to say and then to think that its victims were wholly right! That is the devil of it; the train of evil seems to warp and twist all things awry as it goes on, when once its infernal impetus is given" (*SL*, 3:212). In shying from more confrontational tactics, Howells was not simply protecting himself or defending those bourgeois interests in which he had a stake. He was evincing his deep aversion to extremes, political and otherwise.

II

"IT'S NO USE," Howells told his sister Annie a week after the hangings. "I can't write about it. Some day I hope to do justice to these irreparably wronged men" (*SL*, 3:208). His sense of injustice came to bear almost immediately, however, on his fiction, where the force of the anarchists' ideas was tested against his distrust of radical solutions. Although anarchist doctrine might be "unthinkable" to "plain common sense," he was, in fact, thinking it through in *Annie Kilburn* (1889), *A Hazard of New Fortunes* (1890), *The Quality of Mercy* (1892), and *The World of Chance* (1893).

What was also at issue in these novels was the radical challenge of Leo Tolstoy. In justifying his own refusal to plead for the anarchists, Whittier suggested that Howells's admiration of Tolstoy had induced him—as if against his better judgment—"to take an interest in those creatures" (*SL*, 3:240). There was certainly a connection. In the same November 1887 letter to Annie, Howells confided that he and his wife, Elinor, "both no longer care for the world's life, and would like to be settled somewhere very humbly and simply, where we could be socially identified with the principles of progress and sympathy for the struggling mass" (*SL*, 3:207). That he was expressing these sentiments while living in a swank hotel in Buffalo made Howells acutely aware of the gap between the asceticism he avowed and the material ease of his own circumstances. This was the same contradiction that Tolstoy had hoped to escape by renouncing aristocratic privilege and attempting to live as a peasant on his own estate.

Howells initially discovered Tolstoy in 1885. By the following summer, with mounting excitement, he had devoured *The Cossacks, Anna Karenina, My Religion,* and *War and Peace,* and proceeded to Tolstoy's stories, autobiographies, and social writings. "I know very well that I do not speak of these books in measured terms; I cannot," he professed in an introduction to *Sebastopol,* which he edited in 1887. "As yet my sense of obligation to them is so great that I neither can make nor wish to make a close accounting with their author." Whereas "all other fiction at times *seems* fiction," Tolstoy's books "alone seem the very truth always." It does not matter where one starts with him; "you feel instantly that the man is mighty, and mighty through his conscience; that he is not trying to surprise or dazzle you with his art, but that he is trying to make you think clearly and feel rightly about vital things with which 'art' has often dealt with diabolical indifference or diabolical malevolence."[11]

The influence of Tolstoy was apparent in Howells's letters. In February 1887, when he was doing field research for *Annie Kilburn* at Lowell, Massachusetts, the spectacle of the gigantic textile mills gave him pause. Although he judged them to be "as humanely managed as such things can be," the mills nonetheless made him think that civilization was "all wrong in regard to the labor that suffers in them." He felt "so helpless about it, too," he confided to his father, "realizing the misery it must cost to undo such a mistake. But it is slavery" (*SL,* 3:182). A week later, writing to Curtis, Howells defended "commonplace people" from the aspersions of those American writers in whom "the very, very little culture and elegance with which our refined people have overlaid themselves seems to have hardened their hearts against the common people: they seem to despise and hate them." In disgust, Howells found himself turning "to the barbarous nations with a respect I never expected to feel for them" (*SL,* 3:183).

In April 1887, while Howells was reading *What to Do?,* he admitted how "very unhappy" Tolstoy made him feel about the "terrible question" of prosperity's responsibility for poverty. He could not, however, emulate Tolstoy's renunciation of luxury and superfluity. "I don't exactly see how this helps," he told William Cooper Howells, "except that it makes all poor alike, and saves one's self from remorse" (*SL,* 3:186).[12] To Edward Everett Hale, a fellow Tolstoy enthusiast, Howells owned that the ethical writings had "shown me the utter selfishness and insufficiency of my past life, without convincing me that Tolstoi offers quite the true solution. To work for others, yes; but to work with my hands, I'm not sure, seeing that I'm now fifty, awkward and fat." But Tolstoy had nonetheless freed Howells by "flooring" him: "Never again can I be a snob; my soul is at least my own henceforth" (*SL,* 3:189).

As Howells asserted in an October 1888 letter to Henry James, he was "not in a very good humor with 'America,'" which now seemed "the most grotesquely illogical thing under the sun." Whatever James might think of his old friend, Howells seemed to be shocking himself by his declaration that "after fifty years of optimistic content with 'civilization' and its ability to come out all right in the end, I now abhor it, and feel that it is coming out all wrong in the end, unless it bases itself anew on a real equality." Then, in a oscillation from the "audacity" of such "social ideas," Howells added ironically: "Meantime, I wear a fur-lined overcoat, and live in all the luxury my money can buy" (*SL*, 3:231).

Such self-deprecation was entirely characteristic; it reflected Howells's skepticism of extremes as well as his cognizance of personal imperfections. Howells later joked to his father that he and Samuel Clemens, along with their wives, were "all of accord in our way of thinking: that is, we are theoretical socialists, and practical aristocrats. But it is a comfort to be right theoretically, and to be ashamed of one's self practically" (*SL*, 3:271). Writing to Hale, he linked his pessimism about social conditions to awareness of his own "prejudices, passions, follies," which he believed could be surmounted only by "unselfishness" and an "immediate altruism dealing with what now is." The maddening dilemma was how to translate these ideals into action: "Words, words, words! How to make them things, deeds,—you have the secret of that; with me they only breed more words" (*SL*, 3:233).

Howells immersed himself in radical literature and, to a degree, in socialist politics. Had there been a labor party "embodying any practical ideas" (*SL*, 3:223), he would have voted with it. In January 1888, he told Hamlin Garland that although he would not join Henry George's Single Tax crusade, he had been "reading and thinking about questions that carry me beyond myself and my miserable literary idolatries of the past" (*SL*, 3:215). He was especially attracted to Laurence Gronlund's blend of Marxian social analysis and utopian socialism (Gronlund preferred the term *collectivism*) in *Co-operative Commonwealth* (1884). Howells, who had heard Gronlund lecture in Buffalo, praised the book's "reconciliation of interests which now antagonize one another, the substitution of the ideal of duties for the ideal of rights, of equality for liberty."[13]

Like Gronlund, Howells felt uneasy about putting a label on his political identity, given the stigma attached to "socialism" by the American public. Former President Rutherford B. Hayes (Howells's cousin by marriage), after reading *Annie Kilburn,* reflected in his diary: "It opens the democratic side of the coming questions. I do not find a ready word for the doctrine of true equality of rights. Its foes call it nihilism, communism, socialism, and the like. Howells would perhaps call it justice. It is the doctrine of the Declaration of Independence, and of the Sermon on the Mount. But what is a proper and *favorable* word or phrase to designate it?"[14] As Hayes shrewdly sensed, Howells preferred to detach his own beliefs from dubious European origins by conceiving of "socialism" as no more "foreign" than the American Revolution and the New Testament. Indeed, as nothing really unfamiliar. "Socialism, as I understand it, is not a positive but a comparative thing," Howells explained in another of his unmailed letters to the editor, this time to the *New York Sun;* "it is a question of more or less in what we have already, and not a question of absolute difference" (*SL,* 3:237).

Howells took special care in this statement to palliate his "socialism" because he had once more come under suspicion for his "radical" commitments. On 11 November 1888, at an anniversary service in Boston for the Haymarket anarchists, a letter from Howells was read in which he allegedly "reiterated his well-known views that the execution of Spies and his companions was an outrage."[15] Henry Mills Alden, editor of *Harper's Monthly,* was alarmed at this report. With permission from Howells, he hastened to issue a correction, to the effect that Howells's position had been grossly misrepresented: he had merely sent a polite note, to decline an invitation to address the anarchists' meeting; rather than renewing his condemnation of the executions, this note had referred to Howells's 1887 *Tribune* letter as his final word on the matter.

The anniversary of the hangings occasioned a rehearsal of all the old arguments; by tying himself, however tenuously, to the Boston anarchists, Howells became vulnerable once more to the abuse he had suffered in 1887 from papers like the *Sun.* He was thus understandably wary of exploitation by those eager to appropriate the worth of his good name to their own radical ends. Not only his reputation, but also his livelihood might be jeopardized.

In fact, as protective as they were of Howells's public image on this occasion, his "friends in Franklin Square" had exhibited surprising tolerance during his earlier campaign against the Haymarket executions. In 1912, recalling his long association with his publishers, Howells supposed that although his *Tribune* letter had not appeared in a Harper publication, it must have been "as distasteful to the House as it was to the immeasurable majority of the American people. It raised a storm above my head, but no echo of the tempest ever reached me from Franklin Square any more than if the House there had quite agreed with me."[16] It had certainly *not* agreed. But the house did recognize some advantages in Howells's social activism.

During negotiations in 1885, Joseph W. Harper had proposed that Howells write "a *feuilleton*" for *Harper's Weekly,* "embracing current social, literary & artistic topics, with story & incident" (*SL,* 3:128 n). In September 1888, just before the anniversary of the anarchists' deaths, Alden was prompted by Harper to remind Howells of this idea. Quoting the publisher directly, Alden outlined an ambitious series of articles for the *Weekly:*

> a powerful presentation of the life of our great metropolis, social, educational, economical, political—as shown in our schools, colleges, charitable organizations, reformatory institutions, prisons, courts of law, occupations & amusements—our

> streets & parks & factories & clubs—the rich & the poor, the idler & the worker, the silly men & bad men & frivolous women—the elevated railroads, the monopolies, the nuisances—& Hunter's Point.

Neither Alden nor Harper doubted that Howells would infuse this material with his "sympathy, his altruism—in other words, his warm democratic heart." Ideally, the feuilletons would have a (covertly) didactic effect: "Possibly lessons might be drawn from these observations, showing the real assimilation of interests in these diverse classes & occupations of the community, with suggestions for the improvement of society." The series, moreover, "would command the interest of all classes, afford food for reflection & conversation in society, & would be largely quoted."[17]

Viewed in this light, Howells's "socialism" became a relatively innocuous "altruism": not political but educational, not divisive but synthetic, demonstrating not the radical polarization of class interests but rather "the real assimilation of interests in these diverse classes." Such "altruism" was topical and therefore a means to good publicity and social influence. Ironically, if Howells's "socialism" was subject to appropriation by the anarchists, it was also open to commodification by the Harpers. While they protected their investment in Howells, his publishers meant to capitalize on the market value of his "radical" reputation.

III

AS HARPER'S proposal suggests, Howells was expected to resituate himself imaginatively, if not actually, in New York. For most of his career, he had been closely identified with Boston, in the environs of which he and his family had lived since 1866, when Howells first assumed his duties as assistant editor of the *Atlantic Monthly.* By 1887, however, he had come to feel "that there is little or nothing left for me in Boston, and in New York there may be a good-deal" (*SL,* 3:195).

Howells and his family had always been peripatetic, moving from house to house, leaving the city for summer vacations, and occasionally traveling through Europe. This pattern became all the more pronounced during the 1880s, as Winifred, the elder Howells daughter, suffered her slow decline.

Born in Venice in 1863, Winny (as her parents called her) was a precocious child with literary ambitions. A published poet at thirteen (in *St. Nicholas,* a children's magazine), Winifred seemed favored to reach the goal she once set for herself in her diary: "to be a great writer."[18] Three years later, however, she began to experience vertigo and other mysterious symptoms that were ultimately to render her an invalid. Treated by a "rest cure" during 1880–81, Winifred made a temporary recovery—just as Howells himself collapsed during the composition of *A Modern Instance* (1882).[19]

The burden of family illness (Elinor too was becoming a confirmed invalid) forced the Howellses to abandon the commodious home they had just recently designed and built for themselves in the Belmont hills and to return to Boston. The house there, at 302 Beacon Street, was no more permanent. When Winifred, at age twenty-one, suffered a relapse of "nervous prostration" during the fall of 1885, her parents began their "wandering about in the health-search" (*SL*, 3:228): first to suburban Auburndale and then to Lake George, New York, for the summer of 1887. That fall Winifred was confined for several months to an expensive sanitorium in Dansville, New York. It was during this period, while Howells and his wife lived nearby in a Buffalo hotel, that he became preoccupied with the anarchists' case. Indeed, the growth of his political consciousness and the erosion of his confidence in America were concurrent with his deepening concern about Winifred's health—as if the problems of his own family sharpened his sensitivity to the unsmiling aspects of the world at large.

This awareness was also expanded by Howells's impressions of New York, where he and Elinor moved from Buffalo in February 1888. The city was "immensely interesting" but nearly overwhelming for the self-consciously middle-aged novelist. Compared to the "abounding Americanism" of New York, Boston now seemed "of another planet" (*SL*, 3:223). From temporary quarters on West Ninth Street, the Howellses moved in April to the Chelsea on West Twenty-third Street: "one of the vast caravanseries [sic] which are becoming so common in New York,—ten stories high, and housing six hundred people" (*SL*, 3:225). In the fall they undertook an exhausting hunt for a permanent residence, inspecting more than a hundred flats before settling on an old-fashioned apartment house at 330 East Seventeenth Street, overlooking Stuyvesant Square. In the same letter to James in which he railed against American "civilization," Howells admitted that "at the bottom of our wicked hearts we all like New York" (*SL*, 3:232). The novelist was soon at home in various clubs and social circles, and he enjoyed informal dinners at Moretti's, where the literati gathered.

The family now included Winifred again. She had rejoined her parents and her younger siblings (John and Mildred) after her release from Dansville in the spring of 1888. The sanitorium had proved to be worse than ineffectual; it had reinforced, her father thought, "every bad habit of invalidism" (*SL*, 3:226). Home care in New York and then near the sea at Little Nahant, Massachusetts, worked no better. It is impossible at a century's remove to be certain about any diagnosis, but Winifred's case seems to fit the picture of "anorexia nervosa" that was then first being drawn by European physicians.[20]

As Winifred would reach plateaus of stable weakness and then sink again into vales of depression, her parents alternated between hope and dejection. For all of his devotion to his daughter, Howells sometimes betrayed frustration with her helplessness. "She has fairly baffled us, and has almost worn her mother out," Howells complained to his father in November 1888. "There are some proofs that she suffers little or no pain, but she manages to work upon our sympathy so that we are powerless to carry out our plans for her good." The latest such plan, which the Howellses did carry out, was to enlist the services of Dr. S. Weir Mitchell, the inventor of the rest cure and the most distinguished psychiatrist in America. Winifred would be sent to Mitchell's clinic in Philadelphia. "It will be a fearfully costly experiment,—perhaps $2000 in all—but we *must* make it, or else let her slide into dementia and death. Of course we are glad that Mitchell will even try to do anything for her, but we are not very hopeful" (*SL*, 3:235).

Elinor Howells, it seems, reluctantly yielded to her husband "in all the details of this last attempt to restore Winny to health" (*SL*, 3:249 n). When Howells personally delivered his daughter to Mitchell, he was anxious to put the best face on a desperate situation. "If you could once see Dr. Mitchell," he wrote to his father, offering the same reassurances he had probably given Elinor, "you would see how he differed from all other specialists, and would not have a doubt but she was in the best and wisest and kindest hands in the world. He did not conceal from me that he thought it a very difficult case; her hypochondriacal illusions and obstinacy in her physiological theories complicate it badly; but everything that can be done will be done, 'As if she were my own daughter,' he said" (*SL*, 3:235n).

Convinced that Winifred's illness was hysterical, Mitchell tried to undermine her own stubborn belief in a somatic etiology of her problems through a combination, standard to the rest cure, of forced feeding and psychological persuasion. Early in 1889, the doctor reported that Winifred was "in a very good way physically" but that "she still continues rebellious, and wont admit that she's at all better, though she has gained fifteen pounds, and is able to do anything she likes."[21] During a visit the following month, Howells too was encouraged by Winifred's appearance, but disturbed by the persistence of her "hypochondria."

Once she had gained twenty pounds, Winifred was transferred to Merchantville, Pennsylvania, where Mitchell maintained a rural retreat for patients on the mend. There, in her twenty-sixth year, she died on 2 March 1889, the day after her father's fifty-second birthday.[22]

"The blow came with terrible suddenness, when we were hoping so much and fearing nothing less than what happened," Howells reflected (*SL*, 3:249). In the stupor of grief, he struggled to comprehend the death of Winifred—with "her gentleness, her divine intelligence, the loveliness of her most angelic character, and the beauty of her patient wisdom"—as anything other than the senseless slaughter of innocence. "As I can conceive of no hate that could have framed a law so dreadful as the law of death," he told an old friend, "I must believe that Love did it" (*SL*, 3:250).

Blaming himself for Winifred's tragedy, her father was haunted by grotesque dreams. In one of them, he shared the fate of the Chicago anarchists: "Last night I was to be hanged for something, and I had a chance to escape; but I reflected,

'No, I am tired of living; and it's only a moment's wrench, and then I shall be with *her*' " (*SL*, 3:270). The dreadful "law of death" was even more harrowing than the "awful mistake" of the Haymarket hangings. The execution of innocent men had shaken Howells's faith in human justice, but Winifred's death compelled him to question divine providence. To John Hay, he quoted a sentence from Henry James's letter of condolence: " 'To be young and gentle, and do no harm, and to pay for it as if it were a crime.' That is the whole history of our dear girl's life. What *does* it mean?"[23]

IV

HOWELLS WAS THEN in the midst of writing *A Hazard of New Fortunes,* the novel he had started the previous October with a rush of enthusiasm. But by February 1889, with Winifred "a wreck of health and youth," he was feeling alienated from the mindless and carefree vitality of New York. "I suppose if I were not old and sore and sad I should like life here," he told Gosse. "It's very simple and irresponsible, and hell seems farther than at Boston, because people agree not to think about it" (*SL*, 3:245).

Howells had no choice but to think about it; after Winifred's death, he was living in hell. Seeking distraction from grief, he labored in vain at his desk. "I thought I was never going to be able to get anything done," he later told an interviewer. "For weeks I made start after start, and tore up everything I wrote. I was in perfect despair about it."[24] He was also writing with the printer at his heels, for serialization began long before the novel was finished.

Despite the urgency of deadlines, Howells was unable to move ahead until he fled New York in May 1889 and retreated to a rented house near Belmont. Then the novel flowed "so easily from the pen that I had the misgiving which I always have of things which do not cost me great trouble." As *Hazard* advanced, "it compelled into its course incidents, interests, individualities, which I had not known lay near, and it specialized and amplified at points which I had not always meant to touch, though I should not like to intimate anything mystical in the fact." The action developed "as nearly without my conscious agency as I ever allow myself to think such things happen."[25]

This imaginative surge makes psychological, if not "mystical," sense. Howells had come full circle to Belmont, the place where Winny's troubles all began. She lay now a few miles away in the Cambridge cemetery, and one spring day her father prostrated himself beside her grave and "experienced what anguish a man can live through."[26] He was, in fact, living through his anguish by writing through it, by releasing strong emotions into a novel that seemed wondrously to be writing itself.

Howells later thought that *Hazard* became "the most vital" of his fictions "through my quickened interest in the life about me, at a moment of great psychological import." It reflected, he believed, his concern during the later 1880s with the "humaner economics," the visionary dreams of Henry George and Edward Bellamy, and the "bombs and scaffolds of Chicago" (*HNF,* 4). Although he traced its origins to such social interests, he also knew it was rooted in private agony. *Hazard* became an act of psychic recovery; Howells's profound sense of loss lay inevitably at its core. This loss was multifarious: of his daughter and hope for her afterlife, of his former identity as a Bostonian writer, of whatever Christian beliefs he held before Tolstoy's unsettling challenge, of his faith in American society and its institutions.

The keynote to *A Hazard of New Fortunes* is struck by its Shakespearean title. Chatillion, the French ambassador to the English court in *King John,* warns his own monarch of an invasion by those who, divided among themselves in Britain, have united in their predatory design upon disputed French territories. With a mixture of apprehension and contempt, Chatillion describes the band of adventurers who have swarmed across the channel:

> And all th' unsettled humours of the land,
> Rash, inconsiderate, fiery voluntaries,
> With ladies' faces and fierce dragons' spleens,
> Have sold their fortunes at their native homes,
> Bearing their birthrights proudly on their backs,
> To make a hazard of new fortunes here.[27]
> (act II, scene i)

In the context of Howells's novel, the passage applies most pointedly to the Dryfoos family, displaced by new fortunes from their farm in Moffitt, Indiana, and cast adrift in the chaotic modern city, where they are condemned never to feel at home. As Mela and Christine proudly await the social triumph that is not, as *they* imagine, their birthright in New York, Jacob Dryfoos brings his rash and fiery temperament to bear on Wall Street, where he is determined to attain a position of commanding wealth. Meanwhile, his wife pines for their abandoned western homestead, and his son, Conrad, renounces all earthly ambition.

The fate of such a family had been the seed of the novel. Howells's curiosity was aroused in 1886 about some "Cincinnati men who had come to New York to become part of Eastern society" (*HNF,* xix). A year later, during a visit to the Natural Gas Jubilee in Findlay, Ohio, he was amazed by the booming new industry that had transmogrified farmers into entrepreneurs. "The wildest dreams of Col. Sellers are here commonplaces of everyday experience," he gushed to Samuel Clemens, adding that he wished he could "blow off a gas-well in this note" to give some sense of what he had witnessed.[28] "It was a wonderful spectacle gaseously, materially and morally," he told John W. De Forest. "I believe I shall try to write a story about it" (*SL,* 3:188).

Howells did use "A Hazard of New Fortunes" as the title for a sketch he never finished "about Pennsylvania emigrants to Ohio" (*HNF,* 523 n). But he soon shifted to a much larger scale, more on the order of Tolstoy than of Ivan Turgenev, whose compressed novels, centered on a few characters, had earlier been his fictional paragon. Before *Hazard,* no American writer had managed to capture what Howells described to James as the "vast, gay, shapeless life" of New York (*SL,* 3:232). In taking up what he soon realized would be his "longest story" (*SL,* 3:241), Howells explicitly rejected his publisher's "plan of short stories" (*SL,* 3:230). This project was reassigned to Basil March, who spends most of *Hazard* gathering material for New York feuilletons that remain unwritten at the end.

First employed in *Their Wedding Journey* (1872), Basil and Isabel March were quasi-autobiographical, but decidedly fictional, surrogates for Will and Elinor Howells. The Marches, whom Howells seemed to revive whenever he was exploring personally difficult material, served as the "mask of fiction" that was, paradoxically, the enabling condition of self-revelation. In *Hazard,* the Marches' move from Boston to New York, their quest for an apartment, and their reactions to the city all resemble the Howellses' own experience.[29]

Throughout the novel, Howells maintained an ironic narrative distance from the Marches even as he used them as a point of reference, a relatively stable center around which the plot and the other characters revolve. The force of the novel is powerfully centrifugal, however.[30] Not only does everything seem to be flying off, but the center itself does not finally hold. In a crucial passage, Basil has the vertiginous realization that "accident and then exigency" are the only forces at work amid the "frantic panorama" of the city: "The whole at moments seemed to him lawless, Godless; the absence of intelligent, comprehensive purpose in the huge disorder, and the violent struggle to subordinate the result to the greater good, penetrated with its dumb appeal the consciousness of a man who had always been too self-enwrapt to perceive the chaos to which the individual selfishness must always lead" (*HNF,* 184).

Implicit here is a saving hope that individual *un*selfishness might work to undo the godless chaos by leading to restored harmony within, and then among, individuals and thus to the reconciliation of human society with a divine order. The moral logic of Basil's thinking, like all of the Marches' efforts to make sense of the bewildering New York environment, is inflected by their fundamentally bourgeois values—values that Howells himself shared but that he felt were disintegrating under the weight of social disorder.

The narrative coherence of the novel depends on the loosely organizing device of *Every Other Week,* a literary magazine for which Jacob Dryfoos is the financial angel and to which all the other characters are more or less connected. Dryfoos' motive in backing *Every Other Week* is to dissuade the unworldly Conrad from entering the ministry by making him a publisher instead. Conrad, with his piety and meekness, represents the nonviolent, Christian socialism that Howells connected with Tolstoy, in which religious vocation obviates political activism. Berthold Lindau, on the other hand, reflected the fervid radicalism of the Haymarket anarchists. Howells later said that he felt "a tenderness for this character which I feel for no other in the book, and a reverence for an inherent nobleness in it" (*HNF,* 505)—a statement that suggests August Spies was one of his models. Lindau's radicalism is represented as a diabolical force in the novel. Not only does it breed discord among the staff of *Every Other Week;* it also leads to the death of Conrad, an innocent man.

The imaginative intensity of *Hazard* is generated by the conflict between its ordering and disruptive elements: the struggle of the reasonable characters, especially the Marches, to contain the social and moral chaos that Lindau unleashes. As the problems of the surrounding city overrun the secure enclave of *Every Other Week,* it becomes clear that no sanctuary exists. The novel's "failures" of formal coherence—the length of its opening section and the meandering inconclusiveness of its final chapters—may be seen to mark its imaginative engagement with social realities too intractable for realistic treatment.[31] The narrative fabric of the novel itself unravels with the streetcar strike and Conrad's violent death.

Into the shooting of Conrad Dryfoos and the grief of his father, Howells poured his anguish about Winifred. Like Winny, Conrad dies to no apparent purpose other than to satisfy the ghastly "law of death." Like Howells, Jacob Dryfoos is consumed by guilt, desperate to find some answer to the riddle of the painful earth. It is significant that Dryfoos seeks compassion from Angus Beaton, who is far too self-absorbed to comprehend the old man's need. If Dryfoos the stricken father echoed Howells's remorse about his beloved child, then Angus Beaton, the egoistic artist, reflected Howells's ambivalence about his own literary career. Beaton is marked as the secret sharer of Howells's darkest self-doubts by his fur-lined overcoat—a sign, as Howells had admitted to James, of his own mental and moral insulation from the suffering of others.

Thus although *Hazard* is mainly concerned with the modern city as a cauldron of social strife, the novel also explores the inner conflict of the writer torn between the aesthetic imperatives of his art and the political demands of his social conscience. One major theme is the chastening of Basil March as he moves from regarding New York, at an aesthetic distance, as "picturesque" material for a feuilleton, to recognizing his moral implication in the life around him. What remains unanswered, however, is Tolstoy's question, "What to Do?" Uncertain about the power of fiction finally to do anything, Howells wished that his words could somehow become deeds as well.

V

Howells's impetus for addressing public issues lost velocity in the course of his writing *A Hazard of New Fortunes.* He turned inward and backward for his next two books, finished in rapid succession during 1889–90: *The Shadow of a Dream,* a Hawthornian romance in which the Marches explore, not the mazes of the metropolis, but the involutions of the human heart; and *A Boy's Town,* a veiled autobiography in which Howells evoked his lost youth in the vanished world of antebellum Ohio. Although *The Quality of Mercy,* written in 1891 for a newspaper syndicate, was another realistic and socially conscious novel, Howells's ideas about economic forces came increasingly to be shaped by his experience of the literary marketplace. In this respect, *The World of Chance,* written just after *The Quality of Mercy* (late 1891 to early 1892), was Howells's most significant attempt to integrate social theories with professional practice. In making this effort, Howells incurred a kind of moral nausea: a soul sickness that combined with physical ailments to make the novel unusually arduous to complete.

From adolescence onward, Howells's inner turbulence had been expressed in a range of somatic symptoms; illness was often an indicator of his elevated psychic distress. It is telling, then, that during the early 1890s, after a decade of stable good health, Howells suddenly felt himself to be failing. This sense of decline may simply have been aging (he was nearing sixty), but Howells sensed something unaccountable in the recurrence of vertigo, the symptomatic plague of his neurotic youth.[32] He complained to his father of severe dizziness during September and October 1891, soon after beginning the whirling *World of Chance.* A less severe but more persistent attack of vertigo came during the summer of 1893, after Howells had finished "The Man of Letters as a Man of Business" and "A Circle in the Water" (the title of which figured a vortex). In August 1893, he reported gaining some relief from electrical treatments, but the "shadow of my vertigo" still hovered at the end of October, and it remained an intermittent problem at least until January 1895.[33] Although it would be reductive to suggest a simple correspondence between Howells's dizziness and the vertiginous themes of his fiction during this period, the work does manifest his anxiety over the place of the civilized artist in the commercialized literary trade.

The inspiration for what became *The World of Chance* arose from Howells's desire to revisit the urban scene he had found "so lucky" for *Hazard.* The book he now proposed to Richard Watson Gilder, which had "been a good while in my mind," promised to be "a symphony of many voices concerning Business, business methods, business morals, business aims, business men." *Business Is Business* (the working title) "*ought* to interest Americans more than any other novel of American life"; more even than *The Rise of Silas Lapham,* which had also been serialized in the *Century,* it "would appeal to *men*" (*SL,* 3:315).

Business Is Business as such was never finished, or even started; rather, it metamorphosed into *The World of Chance*—perhaps because Howells came to realize that the only business he really knew well enough to write about was the business of authorship. His knowledge of the literary marketplace proved to be of little help, however, in harnessing "the most mule-like story" he had ever written, one that demanded all his "nerve-force to get it to its destination" (*SL*, 4:9 n). As Howells punningly told his father in January 1892:

> I have had the grippe on me, but I have not got the grip on my story yet. You can understand that while I always have a clear outline in my mind, and generally know what I want to do, there is a troubled time until I have clinched the strong point in a novel; when that's done I feel free. Of course my broken up life here, and my broken up course of good health, have not been favorable to my clinching anything; but I hope to manage it soon. (*SL*, 4:9)

A week later he started "to see daylight through it, where there was nothing but thick darkness. I never was in such despair about anything since the Independent Candidate." But the novel remained balky, and he was having "a terrible time with it" (*SL*, 4:10–11).

In comparing his frustration with *The World of Chance* to what he had suffered with *The Independent Candidate*, Howells was suggesting the depth of his creative quandary. *The Independent Candidate*, Howells's first novel, was a work of juvenilia that he extemporaneously composed in the family printshop when he was seventeen and that ran for several installments in his father's newspaper, the *Ashtabula Sentinel*, until inspiration flagged and the budding author was forced to bring the tale to an limp and untimely halt. Howells later recalled the "shame and anguish" of this "really terrible" experience, which resembled "some dreadful dream one has of finding one's self in battle without the courage needed to carry one creditably through the action, or on the stage unprepared by study of the part which one is to appear in."[34]

The idea of "some dreadful dream," in fact, aptly describes the atmosphere of *The World of Chance*, which begins with its young midwestern hero, aboard an eastbound train, daydreaming about literary success. The story ends, months later on the westbound leg, with his daydreaming about his recent trials and triumphs in New York—until his vaguely troubled thoughts, and then his very identity, dissolve into a blank sleep. "It was nothing." This, the novel's chilling last sentence, ostensibly refers to the obliviousness of sleep. But it also serves to comment reflexively on the novel as a whole, as if it too were as insubstantial as a dream.[35]

The "symphony of many voices" in *The World of Chance* includes an array of quasi-allegorical characters—too many to discuss in detail—whose contradictory positions and colliding opinions (faintly) impress themselves upon Percy Bysshe Shelley Ray, the amiably vapid center of consciousness, whose impenetrable conceit works to protect his mind from violation by any idea impertinent to his quest for publication of his absurd romantic novel, *A Modern Romeo.* Ray is clearly judged culpable for his egoism, the highest cost of which is his failure to reciprocate, or even recognize, the love offered him by Peace Hughes, the novel's paragon of femininity. Ray's libidinal energy, after all, is reserved for *A Modern Romeo.* But Howells, who based this character on his youthful self, indulgently tempers his ironic treatment of Ray.[36] The affable youth is so steadily ingenuous, first to last, that he functions as a *picaro*—traditionally, the central character in a picaresque novel, who (like Ray) remains unchanged by the bewildering world of chance that is mirrored by his passage through it and thus held up for satiric exposure.

As its title suggests, the "strong point" in *The World of Chance* is its concern with the question of randomness versus causality, both in the small world of letters and, by extension, in the universe at large. The tone is set at the beginning, when Ray accidentally overhears, through the thin walls of his shabby New York rooming house, a small-town trader's jauntily desperate tale of woe: how the coming of the railroad to the man's home town wrought not a local economic boom, but rather a drain of local business elsewhere; how the town lost out on a railroad-related factory; how businessmen failed many times over in search of sure-fire merchandise. The man recalls the flier he took himself on Fashion's Pansy, a bustle, which women "kept askin' for . . . till you'd 'a' thought every last one of 'em was going to live and be buried in it. Then all at once none of 'em wanted it—wouldn't touch it":

> Then there was such a rush for Japanese goods, and it lasted so long, that I loaded up all I could with 'em last time I was in New York, and now nobody wants 'em; couldn't give 'em away. Well, it's all a game, and you don't know any more how it's comin' out—you can't bet on it with any more certainty—than you can on a trottin' match. My! I wish I was dead. . . .
>
> I've heard about the law of demand and supply before. There's about as much of a law to it as there is to three-card monte. If it wasn't for my poor wife, I'd let 'em take me back on ice. (*WC,* 21–22)

Although Ray feels vaguely sorry for the tradesman, he has "no great curiosity" about a matter he deems a mundane misfortune, "in no wise comparable to a disappointment in first love, such as he had carefully studied for his novel from his own dark experience." But Ray does expect to capitalize literarily on the "found" material of the unfortunate traveler's tale: "it suggested a picturesque opening for his first New York letter for the Midland *Echo,* and he used it in illustration of the immensity of New York, and the strange associations and juxtapositions of life there" (*WC,* 23).

As Ray discovers for himself, business is business in New York: there is no fundamental difference between the trade in bustles and the trade in novels.[37] Both are "governed" by the marketplace with a apparent randomness that guarantees comparably high rates of failure. Kane, an cynical cosmopolite, points out to Ray, in whom he has taken an bemused paternal interest, that the aspirant author's "failures and successes exactly corresponded to those of business men; that is, he failed ninety-five times out of a hundred to get his material printed" (*WC*, 210). Hughes, the novel's communitarian visionary and Kane's opposite number, later confirms the inseparability of the literature business from other commercial trade. Nothing strikes him "as more shamelessly selfish than the ordinary literary career. I don't wonder the art has sunk so low; its aims are on the business level" (*WC*, 95).

When Ray ultimately does succeed with *A Modern Romeo,* we are shown not only that such success is serendipitous, the outcome of a series of unrelated accidents, but also that it is not dependent on any imaginative qualities inherent to the novel, except as it appeals to the banality of the reading public's taste. Ray's success, moreover, is merely relative. Despite the publicity of good (but belated) reviews and the publisher's aggressive advertising campaign, *A Modern Romeo* wilts on the vine before it ever sells fifty-thousand copies—ten times the sale of a successful first novel during the 1890s, but well below the level of "boomed" books.[38]

The mystery of waning sales prompts Ray to wonder if some higher law obtains in the book market. Whereas Ray's interest in such laws begins and ends with his own advancement, Kane turns the matter into grist for his epigrammatical mill. "Why do we always seek a law for things?" he muses.

> Is there a law for ourselves? We think so, but it's out of sight for the most part, and generally we act from mere caprice, from impulse. I've lived a good many years, but I couldn't honestly say that I've seen the cause overtaken by the consequence more than two or three times; then it struck me as rather theatrical. Consequences I've seen a plenty, but not causes. Perhaps this is merely a sphere of ultimations. We used to flatter ourselves, in the simple old days, when we thought we were all miserable sinners, that we were preparing tremendous effects, to follow elsewhere, by what we said and did here. But what if the things that happen here are effects initiated elsewhere? (*WC*, 360)

Lest readers be tempted to take this reflection too seriously, perhaps as having authorial weight behind it, Howells hastens to undercut Kane by having Ray dismiss his "very pretty conjecture" on the grounds that "it doesn't seem to have a very direct bearing on the falling off in the sale of *A Modern Romeo.*" Of course, Ray's narrow concern with his own affairs does not gainsay the possible truth of Kane's broad hypothesis. But the novel overall takes little stock in Kane's cosmic speculation.

The World of Chance, more boldly that *A Hazard of New Fortunes,* contemplates the possible meaninglessness of human endeavor and the possible futility of schemes for moral improvement, including Tolstoy's notion of Christian socialism. As George N. Bennett observes, each character's viewpoint is "so ironically qualified that even in the aggregate they not only do not offer any useful guide as to what can be done about the general economic condition: they supply no reliable norm for individual conduct within those conditions." Thus the novel may be distinguished from Howells's earlier economic fictions, "which used irony but were not brought to a kind of moral stasis by it."[39] Scott Dennis agrees that "the clash of viewpoints in *The World of Chance* leaves the novel without a moral focus." In fact, by calling all these viewpoints into question, "the novel seems morally nihilistic."[40]

As in *A Hazard of New Fortunes,* Howells asks whether the ultimate source of worldly chaos does not lie within individuals such as Ray, whose disordering egoism blinds them to hope for a providential harmony transcending the cacophonous world of chance. This is the hope that Ray entertains in the closing pages of the novel, where he ponders the play of chance on the material and spiritual planes. The problem of evil, by which we often see "the good unhappy, and the wicked enjoying themselves," seems to Ray to demand belief that justice ultimately rules the universe. Borrowing Kane's idea, Ray complacently reaches the conclusion that "nothing, then, that seemed chance was really chance. It was the operation of a law so large that we caught a glimpse of its vast orbit once or twice in a lifetime. It was Providence" (*WC,* 375). But Ray, whose selfishness renders him incompetent to attain any insight about a world beyond himself, or even within himself, can hardly be taken as a credible voice on such matters.

In his own youth, Howells had been instilled with his father's Swedenborgian belief that selfishness is the greatest of sins, and he never escaped the fear that his own success was founded on selfishness.[41] Had fame and fortune made him incapable of "the immediate altruism dealing with what now is," which, as he told Hale (*SL,* 3:233), was prerequisite to social reform? The most Howells could achieve in *A Hazard of New Fortunes,* as William Alexander remarks, was painfully to acknowledge his compromises and limitations and to hope that "by mirroring for Americans their own complacency and revealing the nature of the society for which they were ultimately responsible, he could still fulfill a mission to men's souls, and thus a mission to civilization."[42]

By the time he took up these missions in *The World of Chance,* his faith in the efficacy of art had diminished even further, in large part because of his perception that literary creativity was succumbing to the soullessly material conditions of industrial capitalism. What the novel finally expressed was Howells's dread that there *is,* after all, a "law" that rules the world of chance: the guiding hand of Providence has been supplanted by the invisible hand of Commerce.

II

THE MAN OF LETTERS AS A MAN OF BUSINESS

GIVEN THE DEPTH of Howells's investment in *A Hazard of New Fortunes,* he was understandably edgy about its reception. Sensing "quiet indifference" to the serial, he feared that the book "would fall stillborn." Despite these misgivings, *Hazard* became "quite popular," he reported, selling "twice as many copies" as "any one of my other novels."[1] In fact, sales reached nineteen thousand in the first six months and topped twenty-three within a year:[2] this was more than double the expected 10,000 copies for a new Howells novel. Such success could not have been timelier. Howells's exclusive contract with Harper and Brothers was about to expire, on New Year's Day 1891. Although the terms were extended for another year, he was poised to enter a literary marketplace that, as he knew, was increasingly dominated by commercial values.

In 1895 Howells agreed with a Bostonian matron that a hit play they both deemed scandalous was "false to the lowest average of our morality," but this was inevitable "in our conditions," he maintained. "It is simply a question of what pays. If a good thing pays, well. If a bad thing pays, well. There is finally no other criterion in a competitive civilization" (*SL,* 4:100). The oxymoronic notion of a "competitive civilization"—in which, presumably, rude capitalist means could lead to refined aristocratic ends—captures Howells's realization that his democratic convictions demanded his faith in a democratic culture, however low its average morality might be.

It is "wisely ordered," Howells contended in the "Editor's Study" for January 1890, that "the divine economy" should have created so many romancers for one Tolstoy, so many poetasters for one Tennyson, and a thousand newspaper funny men for one Mark Twain; "for those who are able to enjoy and profit by what is first-rate are few indeed compared with those who are able to enjoy and profit by what is second-rate, third-rate, fourth-rate." And although some few readers may prefer "to see life in literature as it is," there is "no great harm" in the fact that the vast majority "like to see it in circus dress, with spangled tights, riding three barebacked horses at once, hanging by its instep from trapezes, and suffering massive paving-stones to be burst asunder on its stomach with sledge-hammers."

Inferior goods, then, have their place: not only to set the norm against which to measure masterpieces, but also to satisfy "a chromo appetite in human nature which legitimately demands satisfaction, and which is probably the cultivated form of an appetite still more primitive." The "true criticism" will not contemn the chromo appetite, which has already evolved upward from the primordial ooze of something even worse, "but will endeavor patiently to convert it to a taste for better things" while never forgetting for an instant "that a chromo is a chromo, and that all the joy in it of all the ignorant cannot change it into a work of fine art."[3]

To improve taste as a means for raising the level of average morality was the frankly didactic project of Howellsian realism, whether expressed in criticism or in fiction.[4] This was a goal, moreover, pursued at some risk of confusion and contradiction; if Howells's own work should, in fact, prove to pay, then who was to say if it was a good or a bad thing?

I

EVEN BEFORE the end of his contract with Franklin Square, Howells entertained alternative offers for his services. First to come calling was S. S. McClure, the owner of a prosperous newspaper syndicate and the type of a new breed of publishing magnate, with deep pockets and imperial designs on the emergent mass audience. Trusting his gut-level intuitions about ordinary readers, McClure preached that the "only critic worth listening to is the publisher—the critic who backs his judgment with his money."[5] A speculator in "brains futures," as Rudyard Kipling called him, McClure sought literally and literarily to capitalize "his" authors. What he sought from Howells was less the cash value of his work than the intangible but no less negotiable asset of his name, which long-term association with Harper and Brothers had, in effect, made "a trademark of the firm."[6]

McClure tendered a very tempting offer: Howells would write a serial novel for the Sunday supplements of the *New York Sun* and several other papers in the McClure chain; he would also edit "an illustrated monthly magazine or miscellany of the highest literary character" (*SL*, 3:279 n). This package deal was calculated to gratify Howells's populist desire for a broader readership while it also flattered his discriminating taste. It was as if McClure had taken a page from *Hazard* and was proposing to bring *Every Other Week* uncannily to life: a magazine that would somehow manage not to compromise its lofty standards while reaching down to a mass audience and selling well enough to support its collectively organized staff.

McClure must have known that no such thing was possible in the real world. He probably regarded the proposed magazine as a losing proposition, to be written off on the syndicate side of the ledger by authors attracted to Howells who might otherwise have shunned McClure. Disjunction between "what pays" and "the highest literary character" was figured in the disparate parts of McClure's offer, which Howells himself sensed were mutually exclusive. "I don't see how we could manage both very well," he wrote in April 1890; "the first would kill off the chances of the second" (*SL,* 3:279 n). He meant that magazine editing would thwart fiction writing and vice versa, but he also implicitly acknowledged that syndicated newspapers and high-toned magazines stood in opposition.

Howells did agree to produce *The Quality of Mercy* for syndication by McClure, who marveled, quite tactlessly, that it was "taking" so splendidly, "inasmuch as I had supposed that your work would not attract the million audience" (*SL,* 3:317 n). But Howells never lent his name to the eponymous magazine McClure actually launched in 1893. *McClure's* indeed revolutionized the magazine market, by revamping it along popular lines, and hastened the decline of *Harper's* and other bastions of the highest literary character.[7]

McClure's offer doubtless made Howells more receptive when John Brisben Walker, another of the entrepreneurial publishers, inquired late in 1891 about his willingness to become coeditor of *Cosmopolitan,* the magazine Walker had snatched from bankruptcy in 1889. This time the offer was simply too rich to refuse. Known as "the Napoleon of the magazines," Walker had forsaken a military career in order to make his conquests financially in iron, alfalfa, and print. He was prepared to pay a whopping $15,000 a year for Howells's full-time devotion to "the interests of the Cosmopolitan" and for his annually contributing very little, by Howells's prolific standards: "some short stories or one long story of sixty thousand words as shall be deemed best." The incentive for Walker, as sharp a bargainer as McClure, was the prize of exclusivity: owning all rights to Howells's work and reputation. Their contract specified that "except the novels now being published or which have been already announced," nothing "shall appear in any publication except the Cosmopolitan—this not to interfere however with the production of any play of yours upon the stage" (*SL,* 3:328 n).

"I have a good arrangement money wise," Howells understated to his father, "and work that promises to be pleasant and useful" (*SL,* 3:328 n). In practice, being yoked to the willful and mercurial Walker proved to be less than pleasant, and within months they had quietly parted company, with no hard feelings on either side. In retrospect Howells could hardly imagine what had possessed him to undertake the experiment.

Those of Howells's Bostonian friends who deplored his association with an upstart might have predicted their falling out. Charles Eliot Norton, for one, had been dubious of his former protégé's ability "to lift 'The Cosmopolitan' out of the atmosphere in which it has flourished,—an atmosphere in which there has been a large mingling of the vitreous oxide gas of second-rate vulgarity."[8] But Howells had been drawn to Walker's "very strong socialistic tendencies" (*SL,* 3:328). As a recent convert to Roman Catholicism, the publisher embraced the social gospel zealously enough to imagine a magazine as a means to social reform; Howells too hoped "to do something for humanity as well as the humanities with it" (*SL*, 3:327). As one reporter had it, amid a buzz of newspaper speculation about Howells's unexpected move, "unquestionably Mr. Howells will be a greater power than ever in the radical wing of American literature, and do his great work at less cost to himself."[9]

This account points to the pragmatic value of Howells's alliance with Walker: the certainty of having an outlet for his work without the irritation of continual negotiations. Temporarily at least, Walker afforded him the luxury of rising above the fray of the marketplace and dedicating himself to higher causes than his own livelihood. In having such a patron, albeit one who was a plutocrat rather than an aristocrat,[10] Howells largely reverted to an earlier stage of the American literary economy: to the ethos of "the 'gentleman amateur' revered in republican ideology."[11]

Paradoxically, Howells's freedom from market competition was expected to underwrite his "radical" efforts to reform the "competitive civilization" of which he was himself a conspicuous beneficiary. It is ironic that one measure of Walker's patronage was that it put Howells, the well-funded social critic, on the same financial footing as E. P. Roe, the best-selling sentimental novelist in America. Roe, a writer beneath Howells's contempt, who was nevertheless a thousand times more popular than Henry James, according to the *Critic*'s 1887 survey of book sales in the heartland of the Upper Mississippi Valley.[12] "In an age in which $600 a year was a princely royalty for novelists," Daniel H. Borus notes, "Roe earned $15,000 annually from his writing."[13]

II

"IT WAS A GREAT mistake ever to let it go on," Howells later concluded about the *Cosmopolitan* venture, "and I guess I sha'n't starve" (*SL*, 4:21). There was never much danger of Howells's going hungry. Even without the backing of a millionaire, he held a strong market position by virtue of his established reputation and dependable performance. Howells's booming career became so complex during the 1890s, in fact, that it is bewildering just to itemize, much less comprehend, his multifarious dealings. Let me take 1893 as a representative year and follow the money, as it were, by tracing the literary production that earned it.

As of New Year's Day 1893, Howells, who would turn fifty-six in two months, had recently dissolved his partnership with Walker. Although his books would continue to be published by Harper and Brothers, he had vacated the "Editor's Study" in March 1892, and he had no binding commitments to Franklin Square about magazine publication. He was, in short, a freelancer for the first time since the mid-1880s. In the course of 1893, it is clear, Howells worked every angle he knew for selling his work; and in making the work pay, he neglected no genre.

For instance, Howells's last book of 1892 was a collection of illustrated children's tales, *Christmas Every Day,* the title story of which had first appeared seven years earlier in *St. Nicholas* (January 1886). When he wrote the other four pieces in this volume is not exactly clear, but none had previously been published. The book wrapped something old with something new in a pleasing package designed for the seasonal gift trade.[14]

For many years a Christmas tradition in *Harper's Monthly* was a Howells farce suitable for amateur holiday theatricals. The 1893 offering, in the January number, was *The Unexpected Guests,* one of a series with the recurrent Campbell and Roberts characters, two well-heeled Bostonian couples with a penchant for comical social entanglements. The farce was also issued during May in the "Black & White Series" of attractive tiny books (small 16mo) that Harpers used for plays and other short pieces.

Two additional Howells titles appeared in the same format during 1893: *Evening Dress,* another of the Campbell-Roberts farces, reprinted from *Cosmopolitan* (May 1892); *My Year in a Log Cabin,* the earliest of Howells's autobiographical evocations of antebellum Ohio, originally printed in *Youth's Companion* (12 May 1887). Like all such uniform bindings, the distinctive "Black & White" format gave a categorial signal to prospective buyers, who could easily tell any book by its cover. Since no less than seven of Howells's farces were issued in this series between 1892 and 1894, some faithful readers may well have purchased *My Year in a Log Cabin* under the misapprehension that it was a comedy! *Bride Roses,* yet another of Howells's one-act plays—this one a grim tragicomedy inspired by Winifred's death—appeared in the August 1893 issue of *Harper's Monthly,* but was not reprinted in book form (and not in the "Black & White" format) until seven years later.

Although Howells's work as a playwright was a sideline, it provided an occasional surge of income. In his contract with Walker, stage productions were notably exempted from the otherwise encompassing exclusivity. But Howells had yet to break into the professional theater. So in January 1893 he approached John Augustin Daly about his producing *The Mouse Trap* and perhaps some other farces that "have had great acceptance all over the country among amateurs, without ever getting upon the stage" (*SL,* 4:34). Daly was skeptical that one-act plays, however ingenious, could turn a profit. But *The Mouse Trap* was performed under other auspices in New York during 1894, along with both of Howells's 1893 farces, *The Unexpected Guests* and *Evening Dress.* He wished that more of his plays "could be actively taken hold of so that I need not write so much" (*SL,* 4:63).

Howells's major project early in 1893 was the completion of *A Traveler From Altruria,* which had started in the November 1892 *Cosmopolitan* and was slated to run through October 1893. "I have been working away at my Altruria papers," Howells reported, "not very much to my satisfaction" (*SL,* 4:33). Given his practice, common among nineteenth-century writers, of finishing long works during the course of their serialization, opportunities for satisfaction were limited.

Accustomed to tight deadlines, Howells knew that anything beyond local revision was impracticable once a book was moving down the tracks; complete stoppage, even in an emergency, was nearly inconceivable—and highly unprofessional. And the next job was always beckoning.

The composition of *Traveler* overlapped slightly with that of *The Coast of Bohemia,* which Howells had launched in June 1892 and then struggled to complete, three months behind schedule, by December, just in time to meet his obligations to the *Ladies' Home Journal.* This novel ran concurrently with *Traveler* (December 1892 through October 1893) in a publication obviously targeted at female readers. It was, in fact, Howells's first foray into the lucrative field of women's magazines, a field that reflected the growing diversification and specialization of the literary marketplace.

Howells finished *A Traveler From Altruria* probably by May 1893. In the fall, after he had visited the Columbian Exposition in Chicago, he began a sequel, "Letters of an Altrurian Traveller," also to be serialized in *Cosmopolitan* (November 1893 through September 1894), but never to be published as such in book form.[15] In May, between the Altrurian fictions, Howells wrote "The Man of Letters as a Man of Business." In June he finished a long story, "A Circle in the Water," for *Scribner's Magazine.* Because of its awkward length, which required division into consecutive serial installments, publication was long delayed, until March-April 1895. "I am getting to be a very old man," Howells sardonically implored editor Edward L. Burlingame, "but I hope I am not too bold in expecting to see my short story in print before I go. If you could name a time, I would try to hold out so long" (*SL,* 4:79).

Meanwhile another story promised to *Scribner's* was developing into Howells's next novel: *The Story of a Play,* which he finished about a year later (May 1894), but which could not be serialized until March-August 1897. The difficulty here was juggling the publication of several fictions so that they were not pitted against each other in the various magazines that had accepted them. Exclusivity, as we have seen with Walker and McClure, was a fetish of the literary economy during the 1890s; and Howells understood that it was to his own, as well as his publishers' advantage, to accommodate exclusivity, even at the cost of long delays.

A pattern of publication gridlock was to persist throughout the decade. Thus in 1895 Howells worried that Burlingame would fail to get *The Story of a Play* into *Scribner's* soon enough to prevent its clashing with *The Landlord at Lion's Head,* which he had assured Franklin Square would be his only fiction published during the period of its serialization in *Harper's Weekly* (July-December 1896). As it was, he had pleaded with Henry Loomis Nelson, editor of the *Weekly,* to overlook the simultaneous appearance of *An Open-Eyed Conspiracy* in the *Century* (July-October 1896) on the somewhat specious grounds that this was a short work and therefore did not count as competition. Ultimately, *The Story of a Play* was put off until 1897, three years after its completion. This postponement in turn forced Howells to delay publication of *Ragged Lady* in order to fulfill another of his exclusivity agreements, this one with Margaret E. Sangster, editor of *Harper's Bazar.* Although Howells first proposed *Ragged Lady* to Sangster in June 1895, the novel was not started until a year later and, after many interruptions, not finished until November 1897 (and then held up for its serial run until July-November 1898).[16]

The book appearance of *My Year in a Log Cabin* in 1893 may have prompted Howells, who was racking his brain for any salable idea, to consider reviving an abandoned project from the late 1860s: what eventually became *New Leaf Mills* (1913), a thinly fictionalized version of his log-cabin year in a utopian community. In February 1893, he was thinking about doing this story for Burlingame, who had recently commissioned "The Country Printer"—a filiopious tribute to the frontier journalism of William Cooper Howells—as the lead article (May 1893) in a *Scribner's* series on "Men's Occupations." A more immediate impetus to the log-cabin narrative was the writing during February and March 1893 of *My Literary Passions* in fifteen installments for the *Ladies' Home Journal* (serialized December 1893 through March 1895).[17] The job went very smoothly. Blending criticism with autobiography proved to be "very amusing" and generically "novel" (*SL,* 4:39). In unearthing memories of his youth, Howells was experimenting with a species of free association: "The selection is rather puzzling, but I let myself *go,* somewhat, and trust to what comes first." Still, he preferred writing fiction because then "I feel quite free, and have no sense of trenching upon my own intimacy" (*SL,* 4:38).

Howells tapped the vein of reminiscence not only for reflections on his boyhood reading, but also for recollections of his pilgrimage to the shrines of Eastern culture in 1860. This project sprang from a conversation with Norton late in 1892.[18] As plans ripened for "a Personal History of American Literature for the thirty years I have been part of it" (*SL,* 4:25), Howells entered into negotiations with the Harpers. Discussion broke down when they insisted that a new department in one of their magazines would be the best vehicle for the series. Howells preferred to spin out the essays at his own pace and discretion. But they soon came to terms—*Howells's* terms—late in February 1893; by August he had drafted "My First Visit to New England," the first chapter of what became *Literary Friends and Acquaintance* (1900).[19]

March 1893 saw the book publication of *The World of Chance* (written between August 1891 and February 1892 and serialized in *Harper's Monthly* during 1892), as well as the magazine publication of nine poems, collectively titled "Monochromes," that were later collected in *Stops of Various Quills* (1895).[20] Also in March 1893 Howells was peddling a list of potential short stories to Richard Watson Gilder, editor of the *Century.* But, as mentioned in the Introduction, Howells took offense at Gilder's desire for a contractual loophole, and no agreement was reached.

The dealings with Gilder and Burlingame, in which magazine contributions were discussed and sometimes sold merely on the basis of treatments or scenarios, show Howells operating comfortably within what Christopher P. Wilson has called the " 'anticipatory' ethos" of fin de siècle publishing.[21] The consolidation of power in the hands of editors and publishers after the Civil War led them to act more and more proactively, sometimes reversing the traditional relations between author and publisher, such that the latter initiated specific projects and then hired writers to execute them. As early as *The Rise of Silas Lapham,* serialized in the *Century* during 1884–85, Howells had provided an outline of the novel in advance of its acceptance—or, indeed, of its composition. He had done the same more recently with *The Quality of Mercy,* as McClure routinely signed contracts on the basis of synopses. Such publishing practices allowed the busy Howells to work far more efficiently for knowing in advance what was worth pursuing.

Howells was so busy during March 1893 that he had no time for a novel he had received, on Hamlin Garland's recommendation, from an unknown young writer named Stephen Crane. Painfully hanging on Howells's verdict, Crane despairingly inquired soon after sending the book: "Having received no reply I must decide then that you think it a wretched thing?" (*SL,* 4:45 n). Howells mercifully hastened to read *Maggie: A Girl of the Streets,* met with the author, and became Crane's chief advocate. Later in the year Howells used his influence to boost the fortunes of another first novel: in a career-making notice of Henry Blake Fuller's *The Cliff-Dwellers.* "I did not wait for you to say you were sorry you had not met me in Chicago, before firing off my gun in honor of your achievement," Howells told the delighted (and, thanks to the review, no longer obscure) author (*SL,* 4:52).

A debt of kindness was generously repaid by Howells's introducing *The Poems of George Pellew,* a posthumously published volume by an unconventional writer and pamphleteer (for woman's suffrage) who once had defended Howells for *his* defense of realism and of Zola in particular. During 1893, Howells also saluted two literary friends, as well as his erstwhile Bostonian mentor, supplying the preface to a new edition of Garland's *Main-Travelled Roads,*[22] and writing an appreciative review of Norton's edition of the *Letters of James Russell Lowell.* To H. H. Boyesen, a former protégé, he gave a long and intimate interview, published in the June *McClure's.*

An inventory of Howells's production for 1893 shows an astounding array of projects at various stages of completion:

Four novels, consisting of one book (*The World of Chance*), two serials (*The Coast of Bohemia, A Traveler From Altruria*), and one partial draft (*The Story of a Play*)

One long story written ("The Circle in the Water")

One book of criticism/autobiography written and serialized (*My Literary Passions*)

Four autobiographical pieces, including one book (*My Year in a Log Cabin*), two published essays ("The Country Printer," "Niagara, First and Last"), and one essay in draft ("My First Visit to New England")

Three plays, consisting of one book (*Evening Dress*), one serial and book (*The Unexpected Guests*), and one serial (*Bride Roses*)
One children's book (*Christmas Every Day and Other Stories*)
Eleven poems published and three poems musically arranged
One major essay ("The Man of Letters as a Man of Business")
Two book reviews and two prefaces to books by other writers
One interview and two miscellaneous published letters.

Not counted here are dozens of ordinary letters, both on business and personal matters, including Howells's faithful weekly correspondence with his father and/or sisters. And in December he found time to contribute to *McClure's* celebrity symposium on the prospects for the new year.

III

WITH HIS OWN career steaming along on a rising tide of income, Howells's own prospects were enviably bright. Late in March 1893, he calculated in his notebook that current contracts with eight different publishers were worth nearly $30,000—exactly double what he had earned in 1891 from his contributions to Harper magazines.[23] According to Edwin H. Cady, Howells was making money "at a rate which, what with taxes and successive inflations, was probably the real equivalent of $100,000 a year in 1958" (nearly five times that sum in 1991 dollars). In spite of hard times (the Panic of 1893) and heavy expenses, including the support of several family members, Howells's net worth mounted "from $60,000 in 1890 to $68,000 in 1892, $84,000 in 1894, $93,000 in 1897." (Translated into 1991 dollars, these figures become $900,000 in 1890, $1,000,000 in 1892, $1.3 million in 1894, $1.5 million in 1897.)[24] Although he had some investments, including real estate in Cambridge, "almost all of this had been earned with his pen, and the continuance of his prosperity depended on it."[25]

If the gross income figures are examined more closely, it becomes clearer what were the sources of Howells's burgeoning wealth. First, his earlier books, most of which had fallen under the control of Houghton Mifflin Company in Boston, were yielding two to three thousand dollars a year, thanks to an 1889 contract that stipulated a 20 percent royalty on hardcover books and slightly less for plays and paperback editions. Second, the terms of a new contract Howells signed with Harper and Brothers in 1892 gave them first refusal on all his books (they never refused one) and guaranteed Howells a 20 percent royalty on the first five thousand copies and 25 percent thereafter. In addition, his payment for novels published by the Harpers since 1888 (that is, since *Annie Kilburn*) became a uniform 20 percent, a marked increase over the previous rate of 12.5 percent.[26] Franklin Square, which ordinarily paid 10 percent on a novel selling for $1.50, was prepared to go so high for Howells not only because he was a known quantity (the house earned no profits from three-quarters of the novels it published), but also because he paid for and subsequently owned the stereotype plates used to print all editions of his books.[27]

Howells did not hesitate to press for even better terms from Franklin Square. As Borus says, "Howells spent much of the 1890s attempting to persuade the Harper management to waive the terms of his contract. His correspondence with them constantly tested the limits of his right to place his material elsewhere."[28] But the contract also provided stability in a volatile market. When *A Traveler From Altruria* had finished its serial run in *Cosmopolitan,* Walker wanted to handle book publication; he projected a huge first printing of fifty thousand. Not nearly so sanguine about the book's prospects, Howells took comfort that his contract with the Harpers "would forbid my dealing with him for the republication" (*SL,* 4:54). Such caution was vindicated: after publication by Harper and Brothers in 1894, in a small edition of twenty-five hundred copies, there was no call for a reprint of *Traveler* until 1908, and only then to exploit the revival of Altruria the previous year in *Through the Eye of the Needle.*

Frank Norris once suggested that the big money for American writers, if attainable at all, lay in multiple sales of the same material. In principle, a single item might be used several different ways, making a tidy profit each time: magazine or newspaper serialization; American and foreign book editions; cheap reprints in cloth and paper; inclusion in the Tauchnitz Library; possibly stage production.[29] Howells exploited all these outlets, but the engine of the gravy train was serialization. A writer's best opportunity lay with the vast array of magazines within an exploding publishing industry in which profits were so widely dispersed that Harper and Brothers, the largest house, never controlled more than 2 percent of the market.[30] As Howells remarked in "The Man of Business as a Man of Letters," "the prosperity of the magazines has given a whole class existence which, as a class, was wholly unknown among us before the Civil War"; that is, the class of authors who now "live prettily enough, by the sale of the serial publication of their writings to the magazines."[31]

It is not surprising, then, that once Howells had moved beyond Franklin Square, fierce bidding for his serial wares pushed his rates up and up. While *My Literary Passions* alone earned $10,000 from the *Ladies' Home Journal,* even such small fry as "The Country Printer" was worth $75 a page (or 10 cents a word) from *Scribner's* (*SL,* 4:27n).[32] Although they failed to settle on other terms, Gilder and Howells concurred that a story for the *Century* would sell at the same rate: $2,250 for thirty pages (*SL,* 4:45). For *The Story of a Play,* Burlingame agreed to pay $67.50 for an estimated sixty *Scribner's* pages, a total of $4,050. A year later, in 1895, Howells received $7,500 from *Harper's Weekly*—roughly 6 cents a word—for serial rights to *The Landlord at Lion's Head;* and he expected the same for what became *Their Silver Wedding Journey* (*SL,* 4:151).

Although Howells was certainly among the most highly respected and best remunerated writers in Victorian America, he was far from the most successful in purely commercial terms.[33] When the *Bookman* created the best-seller list in 1895, this index of capricious public favor was symptomatic of the gold-rush mentality among a horde of publishers vying to shout "Eureka" over a literary flash-in-the-pan. The boom or bust cycles of best-seller book publishing were irrelevant to writers such as Howells, whose career was founded on a different model altogether: one dependent on the combination and coordination of serial and book publication.

To some extent, the book and magazine markets were parallel universes. No one could live by profits from books alone, Howells asserted, "unless he wrote a book that we could not recognize as a work of literature" (*ML*, 7). That is, a novel appealing to the lowest average of morality: "if a book is vulgar enough in sentiment, and crude enough in taste, and flashy enough in incident, or, better or worse still, if it is a bit hot in the mouth, and promises impropriety if not indecency, there is a very fair chance of its success" (*ML*, 13). While many a "factitious and fallacious literary reputation" has been built on steamy best-selling books, what *is* recognizable as literature has been saved by the "high office" of the magazines, "which are not only the best means of living, but of outliving, with the author; they are both bread and fame to him" (*ML*, 10). This double blessing of a good income and a good conscience descends upon the novelist because "story-telling is now a fairly recognized trade, and the story-teller has a money-standing in the economic world." Unfortunately, workers in other literary vineyards—poets, playwrights, essayists, travel writers—have no such money-standing; and even novelists lack the respectability of those in other lines of business. But some consideration, at least, is due "a man who gets a hundred dollars a thousand words or whose book sells five hundred thousand copies or less" (*ML*, 30).

Ten cents a word was the rate Howells himself often commanded, but sales of his books were typically closer to 2 percent of half a million copies. If a writer were to produce many novels, however, cumulative sales might eventually approach that large figure, while serial rights provided a decent and steady income. This was Howells's own means to "that sort of continuous prosperity which follows from capacity and diligence in other vocations" (*ML*, 30). Day in and day out for more than sixty years, he practiced the discipline of sitting down at his desk (or finding a suitable space wherever he happened to be) and writing so many words. He did not depend upon epiphanies of inspiration; he never suffered "writer's block" (a concept not even invented until the 1940s); he moved inexorably from one project to the next, often managing several at once. His work was always in progress. Aside from the writing itself, there were the quotidian chores of a bustling literary career: deals to make, proofs to read, columns to fill, interviews to give, letters to dash off.

As Cady says, Howells followed a long-term strategy of "keeping the value of his name high through the cumulative prestige of his total career." This approach, which resembled the reliance of the conservative publishing houses (such as Harper and Brothers) on a respected imprint and a strong back-list of blue-chip authors, may have precluded best-seller success. But it gave Howells "security and an excellent living together with freedom to do his own real work as he understood it."[34]

That understanding was troubled by contradictions; although Howells welcomed the literary commerce that enriched him, he detested the business of authorship and what it had made of him. His conscience, as Wilson says, "exhibited ties to values which still thought of literary enterprise as a 'calling,' not as a business at all."[35]

IV

ACCORDING TO Richard Ohmann's analysis of U.S. economic base conditions during the late nineteenth century, capital expanded "faster than at any other period in our history" during the 1880s and 1890s. Indeed "capital formation climaxed precisely in the years 1889–93." Early in 1893, however, the economy went into a tailspin: a severe depression that raised unemployment to 20 percent, bankrupted scores of railroads, and closed hundreds of banks. As wages plummeted the following year, strikes proliferated. The wave of strikes, ultimately engulfing 750,000 workers, surpassed "any previous one in American history, except perhaps that of 1877." Vital industries were affected; embattled owners often resorted to violence; many strikers were killed, wounded, or locked up.

Ohmann considers a telling concatenation of events during "the year 1893, plus or minus one." He notes, for instance, the formation of three major companies (General Electric, United States Rubber, and Sears, Roebuck) that were prototypical of "a new kind of industrial firm—the modern, integrated, corporation." Ohmann points also to the so-called magazine revolution of 1893, in which the new entrepreneurial publishers (McClure, Walker, and Frank Munsey) waged a price war against each other while they combined to undersell and undermine the elite tier of magazines. By the turn of the century, the upstart mass magazines had far outstripped the always limited (and, now, rapidly dwindling) circulation of the *Century*, the *Atlantic*, and *Harper's Monthly*.[36]

Howells had been recruited for this endeavor; as an entrepreneurial freelancer he had briefly worked for Walker before he retreated to the secure bastion of the House of Harper. Howells's banner year in 1893 coincided with the Panic of 1893, and his good fortunes during a time of economic privation seemed to align his interests with those of American industrial capitalism. He nonetheless wished to believe, as he asserted to one of his readers in 1891, "I have been, with hands and head, a laborer all my life" (*SL*, 3:324).

The solidarity of head and hands, of writing and physical labor, of authors and workers is the dominant theme of "The Man of Letters as a Man of Business," Howells's major effort to make "a thorough statement of the economic side of literature, which is of course anomalous, since literature should no more be sold than the ministry of religion" (*SL*, 4:47). Howells arrived at this statement by way of his own experience in the marketplace, but he was also reacting to a wider cultural debate about the means and ends of literature—a concern that arose precisely from the awareness Howells shared of the rapidly changing conditions for writers, publishers, and readers alike.

In the "Editor's Study" for March 1890, Howells entered this debate by refuting a recent piece in *Scribner's* by Edward John Phelps, former minister to the Court of Saint James. Phelps's essay, "The Age of Words," had lamented the fall of literature into commerce and of bookmaking into a trade. In a supposed edenic state before profit became an idol, literary reputations had hinged on merit rather than good management, and writers had embraced noble poverty and self-denial in order to deliver "a message to humanity that has been mellowed and tempered by long reflection, by communion with nature and the higher influences of the soul."

Such twaddle, says Howells, might carry conviction "to any party of gentlemen after dinner," receptively tipsy on wine; but in the light of common day any sober observer can see that the aims and motives of American writers have never been higher:

> They may often have been deceived in the hope of that just reward of their toil which all men look forward to, but they are not writers for the love of gain, at the worst, but writers for the love of letters; otherwise they would have been railroad men, and stock-brokers, and dry-goods merchants, and liquor sellers, and corner grocers, and lawyers: few of them are so poor of wit as not to be able to succeed in callings which men make money by.
>
> The fact that some literary men earn enough to live comfortably has nothing to do with the question whether profit is the chief end of authorship or not. They have a right to live comfortably by their art, just as a physician or a minister has a right to live comfortably by his unselfish calling. . . .
>
> Let us clear our minds of cant, if possible, and own that there never was a time when literature was indifferent to the butcher's bill. Money is not fit reward for it, we allow, and we can conceive of a state of things in which the hope of it would not enter; but in the economic chaos of competitive society, there is no other way for authors to live.

Writers on the whole do not live very well. In a civilization where "every conceivable service from man to man has its wage," it is apparently felt that the author if paid at all should be underpaid: "that he is the only laborer unworthy of his hire."[37]

Aside from allying Howells with the laboring masses rather than the leisured classes, this passage adumbrates several other ideas he developed in "The Man of Letters as a Man of Business." Howells avers that despite the commercialization of literature, writers have remained idealists with a quasi-religious sense of vocation. But even a commercial calling no more necessarily negates virtue than an unselfish calling obviates profit. Any vocation may be honorable; every vocation must pay the butcher's bill. Under present economic circumstances, it is hypocritical to hold writers to an arbitrary standard of asceticism, as if enforced starvation were a guarantor of artistic integrity rather than an impediment to artistic vitality. The conditions of our competitive society are simply inescapable; there is no returning to a prelapsarian state before the marketplace (if it ever truly existed). What *is* imaginable, however, is a society where art is rewarded other than monetarily.

This utopian future beyond the present "economic chaos" would be, Howells imagined, communitarian and socialist. In his "Editor's Study" column for May 1891, reviewing a plethora of poetry books, Howells whimsically but also somewhat seriously prophesied that "in Mr. Bellamy's commonwealth, when we get it, there will be no such ruinous and wasteful form of publication for poetry as we now have in these volumes of competitive verse." The many separate volumes before him "represent individualism carried to its logical extreme of anarchism, and in its presence one feels that almost any form of collectivism would be better." Perhaps some government agency—"a hanging committee," such as the painters have for their group exhibits, or else "a literary tribunal"—should nationalize the production of poetry and make its distribution both more efficient and more discriminating.[38]

Howells does not say exactly how poets would be paid under such arrangements, but their well-being would depend no longer on ruthless market forces. As he suggests in "The Man of Letters as a Man of Business," the poet who now must "use his emotions to pay his provision bills" may henceforth rely on a socialist dole: "Somehow he knows that if our huckstering civilization did not at every moment violate the eternal fitness of things, the poet's song would have been given to the world, and the poet would have been cared for by the whole human brotherhood, as any man should be who does the duty that every man owes it" (*ML*, 3). Collectivized poets might no longer be the unacknowledged legislators of the world, but they would serve humankind all the better for becoming indistinguishable from other toilers in obscurity.

Meanwhile, in the present world, "business is the only human solidarity," and all are "bound together with that chain" regardless of differing "interests and tastes and principles" (*ML*, 4). In other words, business, as the basic economic condition of our huckstering civilization, binds in opposition the separate class interests it cannot unify. Howells's implicitly dialectical thinking here is joined with a strain of evolutionary theory to explain the "transition state" (*ML*, 35) in which the artist currently finds himself. On one level the transition Howells imagines is from the republic of letters to a socialist utopia; on another it is from the affiliation of the artist with the classes under the aegis of aristocratic patronage to a more humane solidarity with the masses as an effect of democratic egalitarianism.

> He [the artist] is really of the masses, but they do not know it, and what is worse, they do not know him; as yet the common people do not hear him gladly or hear him at all. He is apparently of the classes; they know him, and they listen to him; he often amuses them very much; but he is not quite at ease among them; whether they know it or not, he knows that he is not of their kind. Perhaps he will never be at home anywhere in the world as long as there are masses whom he ought to consort with, and classes whom he cannot consort with. (*ML*, 35)

The biblical cadences of this passage faintly echo the opening of John's gospel, especially verse 11: "He came unto his own, and his own received him not." At present the artist is neither here nor there, anomalous and adrift. But his homeless condition is only temporary: his own *will* eventually receive him as part of an unfolding divine plan. The artist "ought to consort" with the masses instead of the classes because God has foreordained socialism by planting the "instinct" for human equality "in the human soul" (*ML*, 35).

Although commonly (mis)recognized by the classes, often in the role of court jester, artists are never truly businessmen except insofar as they must peddle their wares directly. Otherwise they are "allied to the great mass of wage-workers who are paid for the labor they have put into the thing done or the thing made; who live by doing or making a thing, and not by marketing a thing after some other man has done it or made it" (*ML*, 33). If artists are economically "the same as mechanics, farmers, day-laborers," they are also spiritually akin with the One who made the world in seven days: the divine day-laborer.

> It ought to be our glory that we produce something, that we bring into the world something that was not choately there before; that at least we fashion or shape something anew; and we ought to feel the tie that binds us to all the toilers of the shop and field, not as a galling chain, but as a mystic bond also uniting us to Him who works hitherto and evermore. (*ML*, 34)

In this passage, as throughout the essay, Howells "figures forth a broad community of producers strikingly like that of the antebellum free-labor doctrine, the revived America of Populism, of Bellamy's 'Nationalism,' of Christian socialism."[39]

If this community of human producers has been one with the originary Producer literally since the dawn of time, then why is the artist now so alienated from his own? Why do the masses not recognize him? The answer seems to be that the galling chains of business have prevented the artist from realizing the mystic bond. His foreordained class identity has been obscured by the fall of art into commerce, and reconciliation with his laboring brothers must await the redemptive arrival of socialism.

Howells's assertion that artists are simply workers ignores salient distinctions between the positions of the writer and the laborer. "Unlike the emerging industrial proletariat," Borus points out, "writers did not suffer erosion of work skills, sell their labor, punch a time clock, or toil under direct supervision." Even at its worst, brainwork never approached the brutalizing lockstep of the factory or sweatshop. Howells's identification of artists with workers, then, must be understood ideologically: "postbellum writers delighted in the implication that they, like farmers or craftsmen, were an integral part of American life. In claiming that their value was in their productivity, they ceased to be 'aristocratic' dabblers and became useful citizens instead."[40]

"The Man of Letters as a Man of Business" begins, however, by employing the very aristocratic rhetoric Howells had rejected in Phelps's essay. The opening paragraph describes the artist's fall, amidst "the grotesque confusion of our economic being," into selling his work, although the taking of money for a picture, a poem, or a statue instinctively seems "profane" and "impious." The artist, to be sure, has no choice but to be grateful for any interest at all. "Without a market for his wares he must perish," and society will impassively "leave him to starve" if he fails to strike its fancy. As with those who tasted of the forbidden fruit, however, "the sin and the shame remain, and the averted eye sees them still, with its inward vision." Although others may deny this naked truth, Howells prefers not to pretend otherwise; he confesses at the outset that "in trying to write of Literature as Business I am tempted to begin by saying that Business is the opprobrium of Literature" (*ML*, 1–2).

Such a premise would place Howells firmly in Phelps's camp and thus uncomfortably in league with those addlepated gentleman he had derided: deploring the sad state of literary affairs over wine and cigars. Thus Howells's task in this essay was to work against the grain of his own long-standing investment in the clerisy of New England letters: his compulsion, as Lewis P. Simpson calls it, "toward idealizing the vocation of the American man of letters, feeling a sacerdotal obligation to represent the literary life as a transcendent, redeeming spiritual order." Such an elite and idealistic vision not only conflicted with Howells's moral commitment to fostering the kind of democratic culture that would supplant the antebellum republic of letters into which he had himself been initiated; it also conflicted with the actualities of his own career and his intimate knowledge of the literature business at large. He was finally too seasoned and too skeptical to believe in Phelps's, or his own, evocations of an edenic age of literary innocence. "Simply put, Howells could never reconcile his ideal of being a writer in America with the realities—the contingencies—of being one."[41]

Most of "The Man of Letters as a Man of Business" is given over to these contingencies. Although the ruminative opening and closing sections of the essay have attracted the most critical attention, Howells's abstract speculations merely provide a frame for a practical bill of particulars about publishing practices and marketplace realities. We learn, for example, about copyright law, rates of payment, types of contracts, advertising and other publicity, vagaries of literary fashion, the rise and fall of particular genres, and the dominance of the female audience. The cumulative effect of all this detail is to establish Howells's impeccably professional credentials to speak authoritatively on matters of interest to aspirant writers and general readers alike. As Howells icily remarks, "I feel quite sure that in writing of the Man of Letters as a Man of Business I shall attract far more readers than I should in writing of him as an Artist" (*ML*, 4).

The urbanely impersonal air of the essay masks its deeply felt personal significance. "The Man of Letters as a Man of Business" bears traces of Howells's underlying dis-ease about his own career in relation to his political and moral convictions. In writing of the "shame" every artist instinctively feels at selling what "cannot be truly priced in money" and therefore what "cannot be truly paid in money" (*ML*, 1), he was obliquely speaking to the embarrassment of his own riches. While he stressed how paltry the rewards of authorship typically were, seeming to present himself as a representative writer in a spirit of class solidarity with literary workers, Howells unflinchingly recognized the practical aristocrat in himself as well as the theoretical socialist. In his own eyes, as much as in those of envious literary rivals, he often appeared to take after his plutocratic patrons far more than his supposed brothers in labor.

Merely in describing the wide range within which authors' incomes fell, Howells could not avoid locating himself at the high end. As he appealed "to the reader's imagination" early in the essay, Howells conjures up his own real situation as a hypothetical best-case scenario: "there are several men of letters among us who are such good men of business that they can command a hundred dollars a thousand words for all they write." Such a writer's earnings can easily equal those of the president of the United States—"for [the writer's] doing far less work of a much more perishable sort"—and his forty or fifty thousand a year also qualifies him "to consort with bank presidents, and railroad officials, and rich tradesmen, and other flowers of our plutocracy on equal terms" (*ML*, 4).

Howells immediately explodes this pipe dream, explaining that real artists have dry spells and make false starts that hold their realizable income considerably below the imaginable heights. Then there is the unremunerated toil of revision. Thinking perhaps of his own recent struggles with *The Coast of Bohemia*, he confides that "I know one man of letters who wrote to-day and tore up tomorrow for nearly a whole summer" (*ML*, 5). Such inefficiencies of production reduce earning capacity, "in such measure that an author whose name is known everywhere, and whose reputation is commensurate with the boundaries of his country, if it does not transcend them, shall have the income, say, of a rising young physician, known to a few people in a subordinate city" (*ML*, 5).

In view of this fact, Howells continues with deadly irony,[42] a fact "so humiliating to an author in the presence of a nation of business men like ours, I do not know that I can establish the man of letters in the popular esteem as very much of a business man, after all. He must still have a low rank among practical people; and he will be regarded by the great mass of Americans as perhaps a little off, a little funny, a little soft!" (*ML*, 5–6). However "humiliating" his actual income, however "soft" and unmanly his calling, the writer implicitly takes pride here in his business "failure." What self-respecting artist would desire the misplaced adulation either of businessmen or of the masses? The compensation of the artist's sense of integrity is, after all, like the art itself: beyond price.

This unabashedly romantic view of the artist, as proudly alienated from a vulgar commercial society, stands completely at odds with Howells's vision elsewhere in the essay of the writer as humble workaday toiler. And it does not conform to the facts of his own case. Although Howells may not have had a real model for the "author whose name is known everywhere," he himself fit the description of national and even international fame. Even if he was not speaking personally, Howells certainly knew it was utter nonsense to suggest that his own income barely matched that of a up-and-coming physician in a provincial city, however accurate this claim may have been about any other significant American writer, except Mark Twain.[43]

Howells knew he was not truly representative of literary labor; singular success made him shamefully different. He *did* consort at times—more and more often, as the role of The Dean was thrust upon him—with the plutocratic likes of bank presidents, railroad officials, and rich tradesmen. On one level, in addition, he was just as proud of his accomplishments as on another level he was ashamed of them. There's an underlying indignation in "The Man of Letters as a Man of Business" that stems from Howells's sense of superiority to those who would patronize (in both senses) the artist.

Howells knew, furthermore, that what distinguished him from less successful writers was the unromantic diligence that kept his literary production steady and predictable. A key rhetorical turn in the essay comes when, having demonstrated that a writer in principle might prosper like any businessman, Howells argues that the artistic temperament is inconsistent with delighting the public "uninterruptedly": " 'No rose blooms right along'. . . and the man of letters, as an artist, is apt to have times and seasons when he cannot blossom" (*ML*, 4–5). This statement did *not* apply to Howells himself, who delighted readers in all seasons and who seemed always to have a project coming into blossom.

By his own logic, then, Howells's claim to being an "artist" seems about as dubious as his claim to being a "worker": too rich to be a day laborer but too productive day by day to be an artist at the mercy of intermittent inspiration. Howells notes that

> the best writers of fiction, who are most in demand with the magazines, probably get nearly as much money for their work as the inferior novelists who outsell them by tens of thousands, and who make their appeal to the innumerable multitude of the less educated and less cultivated buyers of fiction in book form. I think they earn their money, but if I did not think all of the higher class of novelists earned so much money as they get, I should not be so invidious as to single out for reproach those who did not. (*ML*, 31)

If their sales are nearly the same, who can finally tell the difference between the "best" writers and their supposed "inferiors"? Even more painfully to the point for Howells: who can distinguish—as he tries to do in a symptomatically tortuous sentence—between "higher class" novelists worthy of their hire and those who are not? And what in this context constitutes "earning" rather than shamefully "getting" money? As he refrains here from invidious reproaches, Howells as a man of letters seems nonetheless to be indicting himself for being all too indisputably a man of business.

III

THE MAKING OF "THE DEAN OF AMERICAN LETTERS"

TWENTY YEARS after his break with Franklin Square, Howells divulged that his motives for leaving the "Editor's Study" had been mixed: "it was not only because I had grown increasingly restive under the recurrent drain of that essaying, but because it had become more and more difficult for them to place even in their several periodicals the annual novel I gave them."[1] If Howells's work was harder to place despite the diversity of Harper magazines, then it was only prudent for him to surmise that his literary stock might be dipping.[2] Howells was ever vulnerable to self-doubt, and his fretful imaginings could have been unfounded, or worse than the situation warranted. Perhaps the "difficulties" were without prejudice: the result of the firm's overbooking other authors, or poor editorial management, or logistical problems beyond anyone's control. Maybe his publishers were merely taking him too much for granted, as they had in their offhanded reply to his query in 1890 about their common future.

Then, after S. S. McClure had approached him about a serial novel for the newspaper syndicate, Howells dutifully asked Harper and Brothers "whether you have any wish or intention in regard to my work beyond the year 1891." When they answered that no plans existed beyond those already made, he was "puzzled and hurt," retorting with evidently wounded pride that he "did not . . . 'propose' any prolongation of our relations beyond 1891." In view of McClure's overture, he had merely wished "to consider any possible plans of yours; for I thought this your due." But he was "not willing to have you suppose that I was seeking a further engagement, which I should have felt it unbecoming and unwise to do" (*SL*, 3:279 n).

The Harpers professed mortification over their "careless & ungracious" response, and amity was ostensibly restored. But Howells's confidence had been shaken. His efforts to establish himself as a freelancer were driven, of course, by a need to secure his livelihood outside the House of Harper; but in seeking to reverse a perceived slippage there, he also wished to prove something about his authorial viability. By casting himself upon the literary market, Howells could hope to sharpen his competitive edge, dulled by the comforts of Franklin Square, and improve his touch for what sells.

We have already seen the immense and immediate success that Howells enjoyed during the early 1890s, as well as the dread that accompanied it: an underlying dis-ease that stemmed in part from his psychic economy, in part from his social conscience. His anxiety deepened with his commercial experience, even after he retreated from freelance uncertainties and, in 1895, again took refuge in guaranteed arrangements with his once and future employers, the Harpers. Although his professional fortunes unquestionably improved during the 1890s—by the turn of the century he had become not only a literary idol, but also a rich man (a millionaire in today's dollars)—the arc of his ascendance crossed a downward curve in his imaginative powers. By the time Howells had been installed as "The Dean of American Letters," he was largely exhausted as a writer.

I

"I HAVE BEGUN my department in Harper's Weekly," Howells announced to his sister Aurelia on 21 April 1895, "and I think I shall really enjoy doing it." The department was "Life and Letters," a forum designed for Howells to hold forth on all things literary. If the publishers were pleased to return their wayward author to the fold, he was relieved to revisit familiar surroundings. His security was counterpart to their exclusivity. "I find that as I grow older," he continued, "I am anxious to have a foothold somewhere, and hereafter I shall try to confine my writing to the Harper periodicals. It has been trying for me of late to place my work, and though I shall now have to do more work, I shall be less anxious" (*SL*, 4:103).

Two months earlier, Elinor Howells had confided to her sister-in-law that although Will was "working hard, as usual," he was dismayed "that every magazine, except Harper, has refused a story or even a paper from him saying they are full for two years to come." By 1895, that is, Howells was outstripping the capacity of the magazine market to absorb his prolific freelance output. The Harpers came to the rescue just when the Howellses feared being forced economically "to step down and out."[3]

Howells did, in fact, stick closely to Franklin Square throughout the later 1890s; nearly all his fiction and non-fiction alike first appeared in one or another house organ. "Life and Letters" ran frequently (but not weekly)—over ninety columns in three years—until early 1898, when Howells opened a similar department in the British journal *Literature.* His contract with *Harper's Weekly,* renewed from year to year, stipulated $100 a week for essays of not fewer than two thousand words (or 5 cents a word). Howells was apparently paid whether or not his column appeared in any given issue; the contract contemplated breaks in the series, with the "joint assent" of the author and editor (*SL,* 4:134).

The regular appearance of "Life and Letters" after 1895 and the belated publication of fiction written earlier gave the appearance of undiminished energy and unstinting productivity. But Howells, as he realized, had passed his zenith; after *The Landlord at Lion's Head* was completed in March 1896, he soon reached the point of diminishing returns with his novels. During 1896 his publications—aside from the department and the serial of *Landlord* in *Harper's Weekly*—consisted of one political essay ("Who Are Our Brethren?"); two memoirs ("The White Mr. Longfellow," "Oliver Wendell Holmes"); prefaces to books by three other writers (Galdos's *Doña Perfecta,* Crane's *Maggie,* Dunbar's *Lyrics of Lowly Life*) and a brief obituary for H. H. Boyesen; one short novel and one short story issued in book form (*The Day of Their Wedding* and *A Parting and a Meeting*); one short novel in serial (*An Open-Eyed Conspiracy*), and one collection of essays (*Impressions and Experiences*).

All the fiction was old work, produced between October 1894 and January 1895, as were the essays and prefaces. What was currently in progress during 1896 were only *Stories of Ohio,* a textbook of historical tales for children, and *Ragged Lady,* the novel Howells began soon after finishing *Landlord.* As he grappled with *Ragged Lady* for more than a year, doubling the time he had allotted for its composition, the new novel imposed a heavy tax on Howells's patience and vitality. So did *Their Silver Wedding Journey,* his other major project of the later 1890s, written fitfully between June 1897 and January 1899. These novels, among the weakest Howells ever produced, appeared as books in 1899, just as he was attaining new heights of public acclaim.

Edwin H. Cady shrewdly speculates that Howells "had begun to live off creative capital—that the ideas for almost all the fiction after about 1892 had come from the previous six or seven years of extraordinary creative richness."[4] In other words, Howells's earning power was out of phase, by a decade or so, with his imaginative reserves: as he was becoming a literary plutocrat, he was going bankrupt creatively, unless he could find a new vein to work.

"There is no doubt that I have come to the time of life when invention does not work readily," Howells told Aurelia in March 1898, during the writing of *Their Silver Wedding Journey* (*SL,* 4:193). A week later, still lamenting his feeble grip on the novel, he complained that "everything is much more difficult than it used to be."

> Sometimes I have to ask myself if my best days for writing are not past. I have written a great deal on the lines I attempted long ago; and I think the present novel will be the last I shall do on them. I am an elderly man, and I ought to deal more with things of spiritual significance. This is what I have felt for some time. Outer life no longer interests me as it once did, and I cannot paint it with spirit, or give it the charm I used to find in it. After this I do not think I will try; and I believe I can find a new audience for my studies of the inner life. I don't know what shape they will take. (*SL,* 4:168)

Always a good and faithful steward of his gifts, Howells had the courage to seek a new direction when he could so easily have rested on his laurels, coasting along the same old lines, now become the path of least resistance. That was all his loyal readers expected, and in changing direction he risked losing them without necessarily finding an audience for the stories of the inner life he began to write at the turn of the century.[5]

By 1900, in fact, he was finding few takers for the old line of literary goods. In December 1899, Harper and Brothers tumbled into such financial ruin that the firm went into receivership under the control of J. P. Morgan and his designated agent, Colonel George M. Harvey, "a small-town boy from Vermont who had made good in the big city as Pulitzer's managing editor of the New York *World*."[6] Howells was profoundly shocked—it was, he recalled, as if the federal government had failed—and his personal fortunes seemed perilously pinned to those of Franklin Square. "But now the House itself had come to an end, at least in its former phase, and I had no invitations from editors; some invitations from myself were met with their regrets for previous engagements." The same writer "who used to have contracts for handsome thousands and the choice of more" found nothing pending except *Heroines of Fiction*, promised before the fall to *Harper's Bazar*.[7]

What happened next would have been utterly inconceivable just a few years earlier: Howells failed to sell the serial rights to his next novel, the one he was building from a false start on *Their Silver Wedding Journey* into *The Kentons*. First he was rejected by Bliss Perry, new editor of the *Atlantic Monthly*. (It is awful to conceive how it must have rankled Howells to be spurned by the same magazine over which he once had presided, turned down by a bright young man who probably reminded him of his younger self.) Then Burlingame rejected the novel, but gently enough that Howells thanked him for "the very kind terms of your denial: an old fellow likes to have his disappointments padded." The editor suggested that Howells publish the book with Scribner's but without a serial. He could not afford that, he replied, "though if I cannot sell my story to some magazine you may find me at your door again with your assurances concerning Messrs. Scribner's Sons in my mouth" (*SL*, 4:249). Now, somewhat desperately, Howells turned to Dodd, Mead, and Company, publishers of the *Bookman*, which showed preliminary interest.

In the end, however, the reorganized House of Harper intervened. Recognizing Howells as an invaluable asset—a symbol of solidity to reassure the public—Colonel Harvey offered him $10,000 a year for the rights to everything he wrote and for his services as a literary consultant and talent scout. Howells also took a lifetime lease on the "Editor's Easy Chair" starting in December 1900.

It is ironic that although serial rights to *The Kentons* occasioned Howells's new deal with Franklin Square, the novel never appeared in any of the Harper periodicals. Harvey, who at thirty-six was, as Howells later said, "young enough to be my son" (*SL*, 5:22), somehow persuaded the veteran of many literary negotiations to forgo serial publication and try his luck on the book market alone; that is, without the cachet attached to the magazines and their higher standards of quality control. *The Kentons* would thus be pitted directly against the same sort of popular fiction on which Howells had long heaped scorn from his aeries in the now unattainable *Harper's Monthly* and *Harper's Weekly*. That Harvey tried to soften the blow by expressing his "extravagantly high hopes for the book" could not have distracted Howells from the implicit disgrace; he knew all too well that the omission of a serial was an unmistakable sign of his "slowly declining status in the literary market."[8]

Howells later put the best face on all this, glossing over the decision by noting that the novel had "narrowly escaped in its agreeable popularity becoming a big seller." But he also went on to admit, sportively, that "the divinity which has always watched over my fortunes, that they should not become too gross and swollen, wrought the miracle which kept the sales of *The Kentons* well within the bounds of a modest prosperity."[9] In fact, despite Harper's mighty efforts to float *The Kentons* on billows of advertising—far more than usual for a Howells title—the novel never came close to becoming a *best*-seller (the idea Howells evoked while carefully avoiding the term) or even a *big* seller by Howellsian norms. Although eighty-five hundred copies were distributed during the first three weeks after publication, interest fell off quickly. The book enjoyed "only the usual sale of my novels, after all the puffing and blowing of the publishers," Howells confided to Aurelia. "My public is a curious one: neither the birth rate nor the death rate seems to affect it. During the last ten years all my books have sold about the same"; that is, ten thousand copies more or less.[10] And the novel was never reprinted.

Even more disheartening than the sales were the reviews of *The Kentons*. Without the benefit of discriminating magazine readers to shape first critical impressions, Howells's intentions were misapprehended by paragraphers of dubious taste and intelligence. English reviewers were appreciative of the Kentons as types of ordinary Americans. But at home "the book has been fairly killed by the stupid and stupefying cry of 'commonplace people,'" Howells railed to Brander Matthews. "I shall not live long enough to live this down, but possibly my books may" (*SL*, 5:33).

Exactly the opposite happened: Howells himself, as a famous author, endured the slings and arrows of outrageous reception; it was his books that suffered mortally as they came less and less to be read while their author came more and more to be lionized. This reversal of fortune owed much to the effect on Howells's career of his renewed alliance with Franklin Square. "Though his contract would be renegotiated several times during the next twenty years," Thomas Wortham and David J. Nordloh remark, "Howells remained essentially a Harper author until his death" (*SL*, 4:196). In exchange for the foothold he so badly wanted, he became a company man who, as the publishers expected, repaid their investment in positive public relations. The stability of Howells's professional status, which kept him constantly before the public as virtually a trademark of the House of Harper, contributed to the perception of his being a fixture in American cultural life. Certainly Howells would never have become The Dean apart from the powerful interest of a publishing power in promoting his literary celebrity.

As Daniel H. Borus suggests, the marketplace had developed ever more and better means of ballyhoo. "Book advertising, literary gossip columns, publicity tours, and interviews all pointed toward the creation of a glamorous person, a person whose life had aspects that were admirable or capable of being envied."[11] Although some writers actively participated in the construction of their literary cults, Howells was loath to do so, either for himself or for others. When novelist Brand Whitlock sheepishly asked, on the prodding of his Indianapolis publisher Bowen-Merrill, for "some expression which they could use in their advertisements," Howells refused to supply what had not yet become known as a blurb: "Once I did such a thing, sorely against my conscience; then I vowed to do it no more. It takes all the pleasure out of praising a man's book to him; one seems to be writing at the public, and making one's self part of the commercial enterprise" (*SL*, 5:23).

Howells was not always so fastidious, however. In 1900, annoyed by the Harpers' languid efforts on behalf of *Their Silver Wedding Journey*, he admitted to Henry James that he wished just one of his books could be "thoroughly put before the public, instead of being left to grope its way." He added that one is, of course, "more or less corrupted by the spectacle of the immense successes around one, and it galls me that I should sell only as many thousands as the gilded youth of both sexes are selling hundred thousands, and largely as I believe for want of publicity—that is the new word for advertising" (*SL*, 4:241).

If at present, as Howells himself had asserted, "business is the only human solidarity," if "we are all bound together with that chain, whatever interests and tastes and principles separate us,"[12] then human solidarity was possible only by means of the chain of "commercial enterprise" (rather than Hawthorne's "magnetic chain of humanity"). And Howells the democratic humanitarian had no choice but to do business with an admiring public that was partly a byproduct of "publicity." Before he could become The Dean, Howells had first to go on the road and mingle with the curious masses of his readers.

II

DURING THE mid-1890s, while Howells was still a freelancer, he had attempted to reduce the demands of writing by finding an alternative source of income. In September 1896, he told Aurelia about "a scheme—which may come to nothing—of lecturing to clubs and schools" on the eastern seaboard and later, perhaps, in the West. "I am consulting a lecture agent about it. If it goes, it will relieve me of the constant drain of writing" (*SL,* 4:131 n). The agent was the self-styled "Major" James B. Pond, leading impresario of the lyceum circuit, who had already made stars of Artemus Ward, James Whitcomb Riley, George Washington Cable, and an even richer man of Mark Twain. Pond had been enticing Howells to seek his own fortune on the platform. Although the bashful author did not think he was "qualified to address large public audiences," he was now prepared to lecture on "Novel-Writing and Novel-Reading" to smaller groups from Richmond to Portland to Pittsburgh, but for no less than $100 an appearance (*SL,* 4:131).

Pond leaped at the chance to sign Howells, suggesting that $150 was reasonable for engagements within a six-hour (later reduced to a five-hour) radius of New York, $200 for longer trips. Ideally, Howells would appear two or three dozen times during 1897, preferably close to home. "You see," he explained to Pond, "I make a good deal of money by writing. If I cannot make as much by lecturing, I would rather not lecture" (*SL,* 4:133 n).

If profit was the object, then lecturing was a bust at first. By late January 1897, Howells had received only two invitations—from clubs in nearby Bridgeport and Yonkers—and he was wondering why. Had Pond received any other inquiries? Did the fee seem prohibitively high? Was no one really interested in Howells and his work? "I am forced to the conclusion that in the East there is no such curiosity," the chagrined author told his agent, subtly challenging him to prove otherwise. "I am afraid that if I put time into preparing papers for next season, I should lose money, and I had better keep on writing for editors who really desire me for their readers, as yet" (*SL,* 4:142).

Having enjoyed his outings so far, the novice lecturer was game enough to learn the ropes and carry on. In March, traveling in upstate New York and western Pennsylvania, he had "a *famous* time, all round." He won an ovation from the largest dinner company ever assembled by the prominent Liberal Club of Buffalo, and he was thrilled to discover that *A Traveler from Altruria* was being used as a textbook in the New York State Normal School (*SL,* 4:147). By April 1897 Pond was pressing for a national tour, but Howells fended him off by setting what he supposed were impossible terms: $15,000 plus all expenses (except hotel bills) for no more than one hundred lectures, delivered no more often than five times a week. "Nothing else would pay me, and I should make any such arrangement strictly conditional" (*SL,* 4:149 n). Three days later, when Pond persisted, Howells escalated his demands to $10,000 net for only fifty engagements: "I am sorry about the grand tour. There simply is not money enough in it, and there is more than enough weariness of the flesh and vexation of the spirit" (*SL,* 4:148).

Howells never closed the door completely because he still kept faith in an economic equation by which talk might equal print. Pond recalled that Howells had "always seemed to reason very encouragingly from a business standpoint, going into details of probable results from a tour of from fifty to one hundred lectures, as compared with what he could earn by writing during the same length of time."[13] The balance finally tilted toward the platform during the summer of 1899, when Howells's fictional output was decidedly dwindling. By then, having polished his platform piece in ten or fifteen engagements,[14] he was ready at least for the petite tour: twenty-five lectures, evenly spaced over ten weeks between October and December, travel limited to the northern Midwest and southern Canada. Howells would split the profits two-to-one with Pond, who would either escort the novelist personally or (as happened) send along a factotum. There was also an escape clause built into the contract, permitting Howells to abort the mission in the event of illness.

Although Howells's first consideration was financial, he took insult when Pond treated their deal as strictly business. In coming to terms with the agent, the author first chewed him out:

> But before we meet let me tell you that I did not like your asking me if I cared only to get money out of lecturing, and implying that I did not care to give my readers the pleasure or profit of hearing me. I *do* want to get the money, all of it that I can, but I like to keep my affairs and my enjoyments separate. I am not greedy for money, and once when I found that people were losing by me, (in my small lecturing experience) I returned enough to make good their loss. . . . You will find me not only square, but eager to do my best for the least I can afford. (*SL*, 4:205–6)

To Samuel Clemens, Howells sounded far more abjectly uncertain. Had he driven a hard-enough bargain with Pond? Was he a fool to be doing this thing at all? At his age, Howells was less than eager to "start out on a scamper to Winnipeg and back," but lecturing could be "a relief from writing, and I must boil the pot somehow."[15]

Clemens gloated over his friend's capitulation to Pond, writing to the Major: "I am glad you have corralled Howells. He's a most sinful man, and I always knew God would send him to the platform if he didn't behave" (*SL*, 4:207 n). By the end of the truncated tour, after only six weeks of lecturing, Howells felt he had been sent to hell (or maybe Hadleyburg!) for his "sins."[16] Having already zigzagged through Michigan, Illinois, Indiana, Iowa, Nebraska, Kansas, Minnesota, and, finally, Ohio, he limped to his last stop at Hamilton, his own boy's town, a physical and mental wreck.

After visiting his family in Jefferson, Ohio, Howells began the tour on 19 October 1899, in Ypsilanti, Michigan. To Elinor, he reported that the ferry across Lake Erie had not permitted the sale of liquor on board; he had been obliged to fill his flask with Scotch, his trusty soporific, at "The Last Chance" saloon. Throughout the tour, as pressures mounted daily and nights grew sleepless, the abstemious Howells drained his flask with such unwonted regularity that he must have taken some discreet pains to replenish his supply.

Neither insomnia nor intemperance proved to be the worst of Howells's troubles, however. What finally became unbearable was the kindness of strangers. Howells was discovering firsthand the maddening logic of publicity: the same devouring curiosity that filled the lecture halls carried over into innumerable and inescapable opportunities for the public to see the visiting celebrity close up. Drawn in by the heavily advertised promise of an author "in person," the public was not satisfied merely to read his books, or read about him in the papers, or even watch him speak. They had a claim upon communion with his "real" presence: the transubstantiation of the author's flesh and blood into a mystical authorial aura.[17] The public consumption of Howells took place in rituals of mock sustenance. "I had to be lunched and recepted and dined and supped," as he told Clemens, blurring any difference between eating and being eaten alive. "The worst of it was that I was meeting nice, kind, intelligent people all the time, whom I liked and respected, and who wished to be good to me; but it was killing me, and I was a wretched ghost before them."

When seemingly most present to his admirers, Howells was feeling the most disembodied, so haunted by fears and misgivings that he was oblivious to any human solidarity. To Clemens he recalled only going through the motions of his performance:

> The mere "stunt," the platform act itself, was suffering for me. I had a five or ten minutes' heart quake in the ante-room before I went on, and then I sat as long and languished under the praises of my introducer, and then I got up, and abased my soul before my audience, entreating them to be interested and amused for an hour and a quarter more. Then I waited and shook hands with such as cared to speak with me, and then I went to my hotel and to bed, and lay awake till I got up and drugged myself with trional, or soaked myself with whiskey. After that came a few hours of blessed stupor. When I could get off on an early train, and escape being seen off by anybody, I thought myself too happy.[18]

The nightmare of "public exhibition," as Howells called it to Elinor, educed an elemental loneliness: he was never more alone than when surrounded by a crowd, never wishing more to be alone than when relentlessly sought out. The misery of lecturing was traumatic. So much exposure aroused Howells's terror of being exposed—as inadequate or duplicitous: a damned fraud.

After a lecture to Smith College women in the spring of 1897, Howells had confessed to his sister a dread of public adulation: "The fact is I find that I hate compliments, and thanks, and tributes. If I could take them ungraciously, all right, but I hang out a grateful grin, which I find stereotyped on my face when I go to bed, and which tires me almost to death."[19] "Stereotype," used here in its original printshop frame of reference, also carries its metaphoric sense. The public figure of Howells, his face frozen in a lunatic grin, invaded his privacy and threatened to usurp his very identity, revealing him to his own eyes as a ghastly simulacrum.

For the superficial Pond, Howells did not plumb such depths in explaining why he was determined to cut the tour short after twenty appearances: "I cannot stand the racket; I cannot sleep without drugs. . . . I *cannot* refuse people's hospitality, and it is simply disastrous" (*SL*, 4:225). Pond was understandably dismayed, consoling himself with the credit for transmuting a diamond in the rough into a platform jewel. "Nobody knew whether you could speak or not, and there was a general feeling that you could not," the agent preened. "I have had the courage of my convictions, and have never worked harder and never more delighted with results." Swept up by his own hot air, the impresario opined that no American citizen had ever been more popular than Howells had become during his tour: "The last week was the best and had you been able to continue it would have been a grand success as your popularity was growing every day" (*SL*, 4:227 n).[20]

The newspaper record lends general support to Pond's contentions, although Howells's tour was not entirely triumphal. Robert Rowlette's painstaking studies have modified the earlier view, traceable to Pond, "that only encomia from large audiences of novel-lovers and awed reporters greeted Howells wherever he went." Some evidence exists of editorial sniping and public rudeness, and the performances inspired less adulation, by and large, than bland satisfaction. There were inevitable disappointments as well: "while many lyceum patrons were attracted to Howells's lectures by his enormous prestige . . . and most paid him respectful homage, at least some went only to see a celebrity and cared little for what he said, just as some went to be amused and were not."[21]

What matters most about Howells's 1899 lecture tour is not its actuality—what really may have happened from day to day as he traversed the Midwest—but its symbolic significance. In the travail of this event The Dean was born. Cady is no doubt correct to suppose that once Howells's preeminence "became increasingly a matter of fact, the temptation to the obvious pun on his name was increasingly irresistible" and, further, that no one person self-consciously minted this coinage: "It just drifted into casual use."[22] But Howells's preeminence was as much a matter of publicity and public perception as a matter of fact; and if "The Dean of American Letters" drifted into use, the coinage did not likely occur before the 1899 lecture tour. One of the earliest, if not *the* earliest, appearance of the sobriquet dates from Howells'sss arrival in Iowa.

In a feature article in the *Des Moines Leader* about Howells's imminent appearance, the paper declared on 29 October 1899 that local citizens "could judge for themselves the aptness of the 'sonorous title' sometimes given him, 'Dean of the Guild of American Men of Letters.' " Whatever private opinions people may hold regarding Mr. Howells, the story asserted, "they know he is in truth the 'Dean' of our American literature and is recognized both at home and abroad as foremost among American men of letters." Three days later the *Leader* heartily welcomed "Dean Howells" to town, and a follow-up story on 2 November 1899 bore the headline, "Dean Howells Lectures." That same day the competing *Daily Iowa Capital* wrote of "the 'Dean of American Literature,'" and yet another Des Moines paper, the *Daily News,* reported that Howells had passed the *Leader*'s test with flying colors: "all who heard him . . . are now more than ever ready to concede him the title, 'Dean of American Letters.'"[23]

The title could possibly have been original with these provincial newspapers (Rowlette does not mention any other use of "The Dean of American Letters" during the 1899 tour). But one gets the impression that the Iowan editors were echoing received opinion, probably of recent vintage, about Howells's literary status: adopting a rhetoric that may ultimately be traced to the carefully crafted publicity his publishers were disseminating as they worked to revamp him into a revered elder statesman. A new and higher tone was set, for instance, in the June 1899 issue of *Harper's Monthly,* where a lavish advertisement appeared to mark the release of *Ragged Lady:*

> There have been published in the past thirty years over thirty volumes from the pen of the most representative man of American letters, William Dean Howells. Mr. Howells deserves the rank given him above for three reasons. He has created a distinct school of fiction, he has made an international reputation as a critic, and he has written a volume of poems which has attracted much favorable attention.[24]

A similarly chauvinistic and proprietary attitude toward Howells was evinced by Gerald Stanley Lee in an ecstatic article about the upcoming lecture tour. "We want to hear Mr. Howells in America to-day," Lee declared, "because he particularly belongs to us and because we particularly belong to him and because we are both proud of it." Howells has become a very "part of our literary climate," he rhapsodized.

> We breathe Howells—most of us. It never occurs to people to hold an Anniversary for Oxygen. . . . It never occurs to anyone to attempt a Parade in honor of the American Climate. . . . It is a question whether anything elemental can ever lend itself to being celebrated. It can only be lived in. We cannot reduce Mr. Howells to the celebrating stage. We cannot get him far enough off. We cannot untangle him from ourselves. His art belongs to us. . . . In his large and sane and noiseless way he may be said to have done more for the self-respect of American fiction than any other living man. Under these circumstances it is no small occasion—the announcement that we are to be permitted, in any general sense, to hear his voice on the lecture platform.[25]

This panegyric gives a sense of the emotionally charged fusion of an audience with a celebrity that Howells experienced from the other side as annihilation: if Howells was now atomized into the American Climate, then he was in some profound sense no longer himself. The enabling condition for this kind of consumption, which Howells took all too "personally," was the formation of an author who answered to the flattering description in the magazine advertisement as well as to Lee's encomium. That is, before the writer who customarily signed himself "W. D. Howells" could become "The Dean of American Letters," he had first to become "William Dean Howells."

III

THERE'S A GRUESOME scene in *Miss Lonelyhearts* (1933), among the most harrowing in American literature, where Nathanael West's otherwise nameless protagonist enters Delehanty's New York speakeasy for a drink, just as one of the drunken regulars is "complaining about the number of female writers":

> "And they've all got three names," he said. "Mary Roberts Wilcox, Ella Wheeler Catheter, Ford Mary Rinehart . . ."
>
> Then some one started a train of stories by suggesting that what they all needed was a good rape.
>
> "I knew a gal who was regular until she fell in with a group and went literary. She began writing for the little magazines about how much Beauty hurt her and ditched the boy friend who set up pins in a bowling alley. The guys on the block got sore and took her into the lots one night. About eight of them. They ganged her proper. . . ."

At this point another drunk chimes in about the female writer who dropped her "trick English accent" and jumped on the hard-boiled bandwagon, hanging around "a lot of mugs in a speak, gathering material for a novel." Put wise by the bartender, the mugs, who "didn't know they were picturesque," dragged the woman "into the back room to teach her a new word and put the boots to her. They didn't let her out for three days. On the last day they sold tickets to niggers."[26]

The virulent misogyny of this scene—not to mention its racism—goes far toward explaining the extreme violence of the moderns' repudiation of Howells during the 1920s (see chapter 5). For my purposes here, it is enough to remark upon the explicit links among women, gentility, and three-barreled literary names. The venom in this rapist mentality is not just for women themselves, but also for what women represented in the Victorian order: the formal cadences of their names are redolent of high cultural verities now cast down by the scorn of these jaded men, who read any sort of dignity as pretension.

As ridiculous as the Victorian authoresses are seen to be, the bar mugs have even fiercer contempt for younger women writers who have abandoned the civilizing role of domestic retirement and all too successfully infringed on male literary turf. Castrating women (so the hateful logic goes) deserve to be raped whether they retain their Victorian stateliness as ladies or whether they perversely cease to be "regular" and attempt to join with modern men in rebellion against Victorianism. In the latter case, there is an additional double-bind: younger female writers, seen to resemble their prissy elders at heart, can do no right whether they go highbrow, ditching their proletarian boyfriends in a quest for the elitist avant-garde, or whether they go lowbrow, shedding their phony British accents and going in for "scram and lam" and "real" life in the raw.

Miss Lonelyhearts attributes what he hears to the men's regressively childish lust to avenge the loss of their own youthful idealism: "At college, and perhaps for a year afterwards, they had believed in literature, had believed in Beauty and in personal expression as an absolute end. When they lost this belief, they lost everything."[27] West does not specify what sort of "literature" constituted the college curriculum, but such men might well have been assigned a novel or two by William Dean Howells. In any case, their rage now covers their grief for cultural values that were increasingly synonymous with "The Dean of American Letters."

Howells's name itself was part and parcel of his identification with a quasi-sacral belief in literature, beauty, and personal expression. "William Dean Howells" must be understood as a "feminized" form: a sign of his membership in the same alliance of women and fellow traveling men that accomplished the "feminization of American culture."[28] The writers in this group constituted the canon of "genteel" authors that Howells helped to establish and to which he himself was later condemned. This was not "Our Forty Immortals"[29] (though the membership was overlapped) but rather a de facto Academy of Triple-Barreled Worthies: William Cullen Bryant, Ralph Waldo Emerson, Henry Wadsworth Longfellow, John Greenleaf Whittier, Oliver Wendell Holmes, James Russell Lowell, and also Harriet Beecher Stowe, Sarah Orne Jewett, Mary Wilkins Freeman, Elizabeth Stuart Phelps, and so on and on down to Mary Roberts Rinehart, Ella Wheeler Wilcox, and Willa Sibert Cath[et]er.[30]

"John Jacob Astor." So sayeth the narrator of "Bartleby, The Scrivener": "a name which, I admit, I love to repeat, for it hath a rounded and orbicular sound to it, and rings like unto bullion."[31] Whether a triple-barreled name invariably sounds "full of money" (as Jay Gatsby says of Daisy Buchanan's voice), its orbicularity does seem to lend gravitas to bare initials.[32] Thus although "R. W. Emerson" was still appearing on title pages as late as *The Conduct of Life* (1860), it was only as "Ralph Waldo Emerson" that this writer acquired his full weight as an American Sage. Much the same was true for Howells.

Although "William Dean Howells" has been the standard form throughout the twentieth century, Howells himself almost never used it, especially before his lecture tour. The following list, based on the still-standard bibliography by

William M. Gibson and George Arms, includes all books published before 1900 in which "William Dean Howells" appears on the title page:

1884 *Niagara Revisited*
1888 *Library of Universal Adventure by Sea and Land* (co-edited with Thomas Sergeant Perry)
1890 *A Hazard of New Fortunes* (first paperback edition but *not* the two-volume hardcover edition)
Pastels in Prose (introduction to an anthology of prose-poems edited and translated by Stuart Merrill)
1891 *Venetian Life* (ornamental illustrated London edition)
1894 *Tuscan Cities* (reprint with new preface)
1895 *Their Wedding Journey* (deluxe illustrated edition)
Recollections of Life in Ohio (edited)
1896 *Doña Perfecta* (edited)
1897 *Stories of Ohio* (textbook)

For each of these titles there is a plausible explanation for the unusual use of "William Dean Howells." *Niagara Revisited,* for instance, was a small illustrated booklet printed by a Chicago publisher for the promotional purposes of the Fitchburg Railroad Company. Essentially an advertisement, the booklet was handsomely produced, and the author's name was upgraded accordingly. But the author himself, neither consulted nor paid, had nothing to do with it.[33] Except for *A Hazard of New Fortunes,* all the other titles fall into one of two categories: (1) fancy reprints, in which the formality of Howells's full name seems designedly commensurate with the opulence of the artifact; and (2) editorial projects, in which the use of Howells's full name helped to set him formally apart from another author. So with the *Library of Universal Adventure,* "William Dean Howells" euphoniously balanced "Thomas Sergeant Perry"; with *Recollections of Life in Ohio,* the use of middle names was essential to distinguish the author-father from the editor-son, respectively William Cooper Howells and William Dean Howells. As for *Hazard,* only the paperback first edition bore Howells's full name; the regular hardcover printing used his initials: "W. D. Howells."

This minor exception, then, serves to prove the rule: Howells preferred *not* to be known as "William Dean Howells"; nearly all his nineteenth-century books were ascribed either to "William D. Howells" or else to "W. D. Howells." Furthermore, once Harper and Brothers had become Howells's exclusive publisher, much of his work was issued in a uniform binding that remained consistent for fifteen years. From *April Hopes* (1888) through *Letters Home* (1902), nearly all of Howells's novels and several of his other titles appeared in red cloth with gilt lettering in a simple arts-and-crafts style. A facsimile of Howells's signature was stamped in gilt at the lower right of the front panel; invariably it read "W. D. Howells."

The situation changed slightly after 1900, when about two dozen titles were published by "William Dean Howells"; but nearly all of these also fell into the categories of deluxe editions or editorial projects. During 1906–7, for example, William Dean Howells coedited eight anthologies of short fiction with his syllabic twin, Henry Mills Alden. (This series of reprints from *Harper's Monthly* exemplifies the publisher's use of Howells's name as a drawing card and seal of approval.) William Dean Howells also edited *Mark Twain's Speeches* (1910), as well as an anthology of Maupassant tales titled *The Second Odd Number* (1917), Jane Austen's *Pride and Prejudice* (1918), and *The Great Modern American Stories* (1920); he also organized *The Whole Family* (1908), a collectively written novel. The only one of Howells's own novels published under his full name was also his last: *The Leatherwood God* (1916). (I am not counting *The Vacation of the Kelwyns* and *Mrs. Farrell*, both edited by Howells's daughter Mildred and published posthumously.) In short, the author publicly known as "William Dean Howells" scarcely existed for the private W. D. Howells.

IV

THE CREATION of The Dean of American Letters followed from the commodification of "William Dean Howells" as a literary celebrity. This process may be traced in part through the proliferation of "signature" materials that literally traded on the author's name. Aside from the facsimile autograph that decorated the covers of his books, these materials included real autographs and signed editions. Collecting autographs of authors and other notable personages was something of a Victorian craze, and Howells was hotly pursued by autograph hounds throughout his career.[34] He once complained to Edward Bok about the burdensome volume of such requests: "Every author must have an uneasy fear that his signature is 'collected' at times like postage-stamps, and at times 'traded' among the collectors for other signatures." None of this would really matter, he joked, "if the applicants were always able to spell his name, or were apparently acquainted with his work or interested in it." In the future, he less than seriously proposed, he would honor requests only from those providing proof, either by "intelligent comment" or bookseller's receipt, that they "have read some book of mine." He would certainly "never 'add a sentiment' except in the case of applicants who can give me proof that they have read all my books, now some thirty or forty in number." Needless to say, said the earnest Bok, Howells's "good nature prevented his adherence to his rule!"[35]

So in 1900, as Howells told Aurelia, he and Elinor found themselves spending most of an afternoon dealing with one audacious collector who had shipped a whole trunk full of books to be signed. The man expected Howells not merely to autograph them, but also to inscribe a sentiment; and he offered to pay for his trouble "at my highest rates for the same time spent in lecturing." Howells wouldn't think of taking any money, and he wished also to refuse a vase the collector sent instead, as a token of his appreciation, until he was assured that the gift had only token value. "Just think of the cheek of the man in asking such a thing of an author!" Howells expostulated. But he nonetheless complied, except that he refused to add a sentiment after the tenth book, giving away merely his autograph thereafter.[36] That Howells did not perceive a theft of his services in the effrontery of this collector—that he could only reluctantly recognize signing his name as a commercial transaction—shows that with all his marketplace experience, he remained a little innocent about the modern business of authorship.

Another arena for such commerce was the growing trade in first editions and other rare books, and here too Howells disapproved.[37] In May 1893, he chided Hamlin Garland for collaborating on such a book with Stone and Kimball, a Chicago house renowned for its artful designs: "My name should not be wanting to your subscription list, but I wish you were not going to print a limited edition at an extra price. I don't believe in that sort of thing; you will have to ask people to subscribe, and that's humiliating. You ought to let the book take it's [sic] chances with the people, like any other book" (*SL*, 4:47). But Howells was soon himself implicated in the production of artificial rarities, far beyond the means of ordinary readers, intended solely for the conspicuous consumption of wealthy collectors.

The first such limited edition was a sumptuous 1895 reprint of *Their Wedding Journey,* one of Howells's most popular titles, with illustrations by Clifford Carleton; the large paper version was restricted to 250 copies. Later that same year appeared *Stops of Various Quills,* illustrated by Howard Pyle and issued in two elegant formats. Howells was ashamed to admit that the "*cheap* edition will be $5, and the fine one $10 a copy!" (*SL*, 4:93). The latter, limited to fifty copies signed by both author and illustrator, was printed in two colors on special paper. Harper and Brothers followed up this success with a limited edition of *Literary Friends and Acquaintance* in 1900: an autographed issue of 150 copies in a special buckram binding.

Houghton Mifflin Company, which held copyright to most of Howells's books published before 1888, also produced fancy reprints of the perennial favorites, *Venetian Life* and *Italian Journeys.* The latter, with illustrations by Joseph Pennell, appeared in 1901, in an issue limited to 300 copies. An even more luxurious edition of *Venetian Life* came out in 1907: 550 two-volume sets in three-quarters morocco, with nineteen color plates by Edmund H. Garrett, signed by author, illustrator, and publisher too.[38] The set sold for $15.00 (equivalent to more than two hundred 1991 dollars).

Although such deluxe formats may have been distasteful to Howells, he had no compunctions about another means of publication aimed at affluent readers. Apparently on his own initiative, he met late in 1896 with George H. Mifflin, president of Houghton Mifflin, to discuss the possibility of "a subscription edition." Houghton Mifflin was the publisher of most of the Triple-Barreled Worthies, whose voluminous standard editions had proved to be quite profitable. Howells, plainly delighted at the prospect of having his own works rub bindings with theirs on the same exclusive shelves, immediately obtained J. Henry Harper's cordial assent to further negotiations over the reprinting of books controlled by Franklin Square. Pronouncing himself "ready to revise the whole set of my books for the new edition" (*SL*, 4:137), Howells met after New Year's with Mifflin's delegate, Horace Scudder, to consider what was feasible. If the edition could not include everything, then it might "be made up of my novels alone, or of my novels and travels," running in that case to some eighteen or twenty volumes (*SL*, 4:140). Discussions broke down at this point, and Houghton Mifflin backed away from any deal. It has often been assumed that financial impediments were paramount: Harper and Brothers probably wanted too much for the use of their titles. But things never advanced to the point of any such dealings between the publishers. In uncovering the internal company politics surrounding the decision, Michael Anesko has recently shown that other marketplace considerations were, in fact, decisive.[39]

Mifflin ardently supported the project, at least initially, arguing that since Howells's "position as one of our foremost men of letters is secure," the collected edition would be "a good venture for the House, and quite a card." It would be a coup, that is, to reclaim an author who in straying from Boston for the greener pastures of New York had also (disloyally) deserted the house that had nurtured his early career. Mifflin reminded his colleagues "that Howells was about the only author who left us in 1880, and now he comes knocking at the door."[40] Recapturing the prodigal Howells, then, promised to be rewarding in more ways than one.

Internal memos suggest that other members of the firm, particularly the field representatives in New York, did not share Mifflin's enthusiasm; based on the mediocre sales record of Howells's books, they considered him too much of a risk. Pressed to justify his advocacy, Mifflin pointed to the huge success of the Bret Harte Edition despite the anemic sales of individual Harte titles; and he stressed the opportunity for Houghton Mifflin to outshine the competition by using "a different get-up from our other standard editions," something along the elegant lines of the Stevenson Edition from Scribner's.

Close analysis of cost versus price led to the inexorable conclusion, however, that whereas a complete edition would not be viable, a viable edition (say, of the fiction alone) would not be complete, thereby losing a major selling point for "standard" editions. The only way out of the conundrum was to combine two (or more) titles in some volumes, compensating for the additional bulk with thinner paper. When Mifflin ran this notion up the flagpole in Boston, no one saluted in New York; by early February 1897 the firm had decided, as Mifflin put it to an associate, "to hang the Howells up." In the end, despite the publisher's assertion that "Howells's position in American literature we all think is far more permanently assured than Bret Harte's," there was a disabling doubt about Howells's being a "standard" author.[41]

Five months later, in the course of tough bargaining with Elizabeth Stuart Phelps Ward (who was using the example of Howells's generous terms with Harper and Brothers as leverage), Mifflin adduced the failed standard edition as evidence of Howells's declining market status. In "strictest confidence," Mifflin purported to give Ward the juicy details about why the publisher had declined "the offer of bringing together all his books for a final 'definitive' Edition, which had it been made and sold by the methods we had in mind should have brought him in a permanent and steady income." Howells, alas, had "written himself out"—killing "the goose so to speak that 'laid the golden egg!' " by spreading himself too thin. "His books now simply don't sell, and he finds doors once so hospitably open now closed to him." The root of all this evil was evidently Howells's decision to go freelance: "He is almost the only one of 'our authors' who thought he saw his interest in the 'highest bid' policy, and the results in his case have been quite disasterous [sic] to his permanent place in literature and I believe also to his personal happiness" (*SL*, 4:140 n).

Mifflin's letter combined unctuous guile with calculated malice in an attempt to disarm Ward with the cautionary tale of Howells's supposed ruin. (She didn't buy it.) In 1896, as we have seen, Howells's professional standing was far from as shaky as Mifflin self-servingly maintained; nor was Howells perceptibly unhappy in his personal life. But what passed "in strictest confidence" here was undoubtedly grist for the literary rumor mill. And Howells *was* definitely aware of his diminishing opportunities. That was why he had been ready to cease freelancing and re-sign with the Harpers the year before he approached Mifflin. The fiasco with Houghton Mifflin was just one more indication that Howells's career during the late 1890s was in transition between success on the old basis and a new form of success that depended on the evolution of The Dean. He was now faced either with achieving new life through a kind of living death—becoming a "standard author"—or else accepting a fatal decline in income and prestige.

There may have been a core of truth, after all, in Mifflin's remark about Howells's "permanent place in literature"; neither in nor out of his Deanly role did Howells become a standard author in his time or ours, and that failure may have been inseparable from his lack of a standard edition. "If it is true," Anesko contends, "that the security of Henry James's modern reputation can be traced largely to the rediscovery of the New York Edition (and its critical prefaces)," then the comparative *in*security of Howells's rank may "be attributed (at least partially) to the absence of a particular form of cultural evidence."[42]

This absence did not become permanent, however, until late in Howells's career. After the withdrawal by Houghton Mifflin, all talk of a collected works was dropped for several years; talk was then resumed with Harper and Brothers after 1900. Howells mentioned the project to Charles Eliot Norton in 1902, saying that "it would take a Vatican library to hold me, almost," and hinting that a "treaty" might be in the offing between Harper and Houghton Mifflin (*SL*, 5:37).[43] By 1906, after prolonged negotiations among the author and his past and present publishers, planning had begun, apparently in earnest, for an edition of thirty-five volumes. With James's splendid but daunting example before him, Howells endeavored to write his own "Story of the Story" for each volume. But doing the "Bibliographicals," as he ultimately called these prefaces, soon became unbearable. "I believe I was right in wishing the volumes to go [before] the public without any word of explanation or comment from me," he wrote to Frederick A. Duneka, his editor, "because they are already most intimately full of me, and are their own explanation and comment." Not only were the prefaces "superfluous and impertinent," but they also seemed unduly imitative of James (*SL*, 5:276–77). Although Howells never developed an opaque "late manner," the prose of the "Bibliographicals" was, in fact, uncharacteristically elliptical and turgid, and they revealed little or nothing of the deeper sources of the fiction. In the end, ironically, Howells flogged himself through the writing of more prefaces than were ever needed. The Library Edition folded after the first six volumes (all Harper titles) appeared together in 1911, a casualty of the competing publishers' miscommunication and intransigence, but also of Howells's falling reputation.[44]

Speaking of good book design in the "Editor's Study" for February 1890, Howells had praised the royal octavo format of a recent edition of Boswell's *Life of Johnson*. Books should be light and flexible, he asserted, as easy to hold in the hand as to slip into a man's breast pocket or a woman's shopping bag. Above all, what is intended for ordinary reading should be inviting and informal: "in an age when all things become more and more perceptibly transitory, the first appeal of a book should not be made from covers bespeaking perpetuity. That should be for the library edition, to come later, if at all."[45]

When Howells's Library Edition did come, at least in small part, he hesitated "to forecast the plumage of our unhatched chickens too far ahead"; but he specified nonetheless how the volumes should look. As James had already taken maroon, some other "richly dark sober cloth" would do: dull blue or green. The titles should be lettered directly on the spine, not on paper labels, and there should be "nothing but the title; no decoration of any kind" (*SL*, 5:276). Howells's wishes were honored to the letter. The Library Edition was dressed out in ribbed, dark green cloth devoid of any decoration; on each spine, within a smooth rectangle double-boxed in gilt, appeared the title and the author's name. The design could not have been less pretentious. Having yielded to such austerity for the cover, the publishers adorned each volume with an ornate, two-color title page with "The Writings of William Dean Howells" set in black letter.

It is telling that when H. L. Mencken launched his notorious attack on "The Dean" in 1917, he conjured up a Library Edition that did not, in fact, exist: "a long row of uninspired and hollow books, with no more ideas in them than so many volumes of the *Ladies' Home Journal,* and no more deep and contagious feeling than so many reports of autopsies, and no more glow and gusto than so many tables of bond prices."[46] The Sage of Baltimore, who used his plain initials, was eviscerating one of those standard authors with the triple-barreled names that the moderns found so thoroughly detestable. But if H. L. Mencken had bothered to look at the very short row of the actual Library Edition, he might have noticed that on each spine the author was given simply as "W. D. Howells."

IV
THE AGE OF HOWELLS

WHEN TOLSTOY'S seventieth birthday was observed at a New York dinner in September 1898, the ailing E. C. Stedman failed to attend. In his letter of regret, however, he seized the occasion to pay tribute to Tolstoy's chief American admirer:

> In my own belief the most sincere, the most modest, the most distinguished, of our living writers, has never been so great as since he openly consecrated his humor, his imagination, his pathos to the service of humanity, though with compassionate tears that almost blinded his vision to the glimpses of dawn. If he is not yet fully comprehended, he is beloved—already on our hearts' list for canonization. The rest will follow. If I were at your gathering, I would ask you to join me in a toast to Mr. Howells. (*SL*, 4:213–14 n)[1]

Stedman was not using "canonization" in its current academic sense (he was thinking, rather, of sainthood), but the slippage from a sacerdotal to a secular meaning was nonetheless implicit here, as much as in Stedman's own canonizing act of assembling *An American Anthology, 1787–1900.* This massive book, the most comprehensive poetry anthology yet to be produced in the United States, was Stedman's attempt at the turn of the new century to fix the reputations of the old one.[2]

Much the same purpose was served by the publication that same pivotal year, 1900, of Howells's *Literary Friends and Acquaintance,* in which the heir to the New England clerisy shrewdly but kindly reassessed the elders who had once anointed him. *Literary Friends and Acquaintance* was part of a large body of critical work, including 150 critical essays and several books of criticism, that established The Dean's canon of literary saints during Howells's last two decades. In his farewell "Editor's Study" (March 1892), he had forecast his successor's possible reaction to the retiring incumbent's literary divinities: "We imagine his looking curiously at the collection of moral bric-a-brac . . . and asking 'What strange gods are these?' when he comes to the little side altars with the pictures or the busts of canonized realists above them."[3] Later, as The Dean, Howells took his responsibilities to include the reformation of American taste, in part through pronouncements on what writers, especially native ones, deserved such canonization.

The force of Howells's critical opinions is suggested by his attendance at a production of *Tess of the D'Urbervilles* in 1902. Hardy's novel had been controversial, and throughout this performance of a stage adaptation, playgoers looked to The Dean for its cues. "Prominent among those in the audience," the New York *News* reported, "was William Dean Howells, toward whom many [opera] glasses were leveled from time to time when there was any doubt about forgiving certain moral features of the play." Fortunately for the players and playwright alike, "the Dean of American Letters was disposed to be liberal" (*SL*, 5:26 n). William Dean Howells functioned here not just in his literary capacity as a supreme arbiter of taste, but also in his quasi-clerical role as one invested with authority to bind and loose literary sins, to absolve them or not.

From a different perspective on the same occasion, Edith Wharton also testified to Howells's preeminence. She too had been present for *Tess of the D'Urbervilles,* and she had admired the leading actress's performance so much that she implored The Dean to speak in her favor: "I wish *you* would write something about Mrs. [Minnie Maddern] Fiske, who seems to me, from what I saw last night, worthy of being singled out by some one whose good opinion counts with our poor muddled 'doped' theatrical public."[4] Howells had already acclaimed Mrs. Fiske in a review of the 1897 debut of this same play. He nonetheless acted immediately on Wharton's suggestion, writing to the actress: "I wish to tell you how very *great* I again thought your Tess, the other night. . . . I thank you for a tremendous emotion" (*SL*, 5:25).

Wharton, of course, had no need of Howells's tutelage in reaching her own aesthetic judgments; but no less than those in the "doped" segment of the audience, she deferred to The Dean's cultural authority. As Henry Blake Fuller put it, on the occasion of Howells's seventieth birthday in 1907,

> I want to record my conviction that when the fussy and noisy accidents of our crowded day come to be left behind it will be perceived that for one full generation in American annals the dominant influence has been yours—and always for the good. The Age of Howells—isn't that, some time, possible and likely? To remain imbedded as a definite, integral and respected figure in the national literature—what happier fate?" (*SL*, 5:213 n).

The Age of Howells, such as it was or would be, was already half over in 1907; it came and went in little more than a decade, roughly from his lecture tour in 1899 through his seventy-fifth birthday party in 1912. At the time of this celebration, Howells's power was already greatly diminished. By his death in 1920, he had not only outlived his beloved wife and most of his friends; he had also long since lost his dominant influence on the national literature.

I

WHEN JOHN MACY quipped that Howells "became the Dean of American Letters, and there was no one else on the Faculty,"[5] he inadvertently made a key point about the Deanship: it was never, in fact, an *academic* position. Soon after Howells's arrival in Cambridge during the late 1860s, he briefly taught at Harvard, and he delivered the Lowell Institute Lectures. But during the remainder of his career he consistently discouraged academic overtures, and he declined appointments at Union College (1868) and Johns Hopkins (1882), as well as the Smith Professorship at Harvard (1886). And although he took honorary M.A.'s from both Harvard (1867) and Yale (1881)—in addition to honorary doctorates from Yale (1901), Oxford (1904), Western Reserve (1904), Columbia (1905), and Princeton (1912)—Howells was never truly "on the faculty." No professorship, however, not even the prestigious chair at Harvard, in which Howells would have succeeded Lowell and Longfellow, could have afforded him the power he exercised as The Dean without academic portfolio. Operating outside of the universities, The Dean of American Letters strove to adjudicate the merits of American writers and to celebrate their accomplishments.

In the "Editor's Study" for March 1890, Howells had accepted a challenge (from E. J. Phelps) to dare name "our poets, our dramatists, our historians, our essayists, our philosophers, our really capable critics." Howells nominated writers, genre by genre, for what may be seen as an incipient Dean's canon.[6] Following the traditional hierarchy of genres invoked by Phelps, Howells began with poetry. Though "the time in which our great cycle of poets flourished" had passed with the deaths of Bryant, Emerson, and Longfellow, there were still honorable survivors: Holmes, Whittier, Lowell, Whitman, John T. Trowbridge, and Richard Henry Stoddard. Among poets still in their prime, Howells favored Stedman and Thomas Bailey Aldrich. As for the promising younger generation: "If we mention only Messrs. John Boyle O'Reilly, G. P. Lathrop, R. W. Gilder, James Whitcomb Riley, H. H. Boyesen, J. Madison Cawein, the Canadian Lampman, H. C. Bunner, Edgar Fawcett, Maurice Thompson, it is because their names come to mind as we write."[7]

Acknowledging that our dramatists "are yet mainly to come," Howells instead extolled our historians: Francis Parkman, Herbert Bancroft, J. B. McMaster, John Fiske, Theodore Roosevelt, and Henry Adams. Special praise was accorded *Abraham Lincoln: A History* by the president's secretaries, John Hay and John Nicolay. Notable American essayists included Thomas Wentworth Higginson, George W. Curtis, Charles Dudley Warner, John Burroughs, Horace E. Scudder, and George Woodberry. Fiske, William James, and Josiah Royce counted as our ranking philosophers. Capable critics, who "are always rather rare birds," were well represented by Lowell, Stedman, and Thomas Sergeant Perry. On this occasion Howells did not enumerate the American writers of fiction he admired; but throughout his term in the "Editor's Study," however, he had regularly advanced the reputations of Hawthorne, Henry James, and Mark Twain, along with such younger realists as H. H. Boyesen, George W. Cable, Mary Noailles Murfree (Charles Egbert Craddock), John De Forest, Edward Eggleston, Harold Frederic, Hamlin Garland, Sarah Orne Jewett, and Mary E. Wilkins.

In his "Editor's Study" for November 1891, refuting the taunts of English critics that the United States lacked a respectable national literature, Howells insisted that "at this stage of the proceedings there is no such thing as nationality in the highest literary expression; but there is a universality, a humanity, which is very much better." And he allied American writing with the "universal features" of literary realism from Spain, France, Italy, Russia, and Scandinavia. Insisting that "for all aesthetic purposes the American people are not a nation, but a condition," Howells also contended: "Their literature, so far as they have produced any, is American-English literature, just as the English literature is English-European, and it is as absurd to ask them to have a literature wholly their own as to ask them to have a language wholly their own."

Howells nonetheless endeavored to discern distinguishing features. Anticipating Van Wyck Brooks's later distinction between "highbrow" and "lowbrow,"[8] Howells remarked the "apparently opposite, but probably parallel" tendencies of American literature: "one a tendency toward an elegance refined and polished, both in thought and phrase, almost to tenuity; the other a tendency to grotesqueness, wild and extravagant, to the point of anarchy." The inimitably American poetry of Longfellow and Whitman could be said to stand for these divergent tendencies: "The work of both is a part of that American literature which also embraces the work of Mark Twain and of Lowell, of Artemus Ward and of Whittier, of Bret Harte and of Emerson, of G. W. Cable and of Henry James, of Miss Murfree and of O. W. Holmes, of Whitcomb Riley and of T. B. Aldrich."[9]

By 1900, however, as Howells was being installed as The Dean of American Letters, his judgment was beginning to be contested within a "new mode of literary production," one that, as David R. Shumway remarks, "produced a crisis of succession in literary—and especially critical—authority." Although Howells was certainly "the most influential person in American literary culture at the turn of the century," and although "no university professor came close to challenging him for this position," it was ultimately the professors who superseded The Dean and universities that assumed responsibility for building and maintaining the American canon.[10]

The professionalization of literary studies within departments of English coincided with the professionalization of law, medicine, engineering, and the social sciences. It was part and parcel of a broad transition from industrial to consumer capitalism, with its intensified control of the labor process, its drive toward vertical integration and monopolistic management of markets, and its stress on creating demand, especially among the mass of consumers, through product uniformity and aggressive advertising. As Richard Ohmann observes, the new universities "came into being along with the professional-managerial class they educated." The academy "was gearing itself up to be a supplier and certifier of the professionals and managers needed by those integrated corporations and by the other institutions that came into being to monitor and service the corporate social order."[11]

Whereas Howells had never found his lack of formal education to be an impediment to his accruing cultural capital, the corporate social order demanded such credentials as the Germanic doctoral degree. Indeed, William James, long established as a Harvard professor, had studied in Germany. Nonetheless—and speaking for many of his contemporaries—James deplored "the Ph.D. Octopus" as a grotesque betrayal of the academy's true mission to be "the jealous custodians of personal and spiritual spontaneity." These custodians were honor-bound to guard "against contributing to the increase of officialism and snobbery and insincerity as against a pestilence."[12] Whatever its merits or demerits, the Ph.D. increasingly became prerequisite to employment in universities, and the professionalized English faculty soon took over the business of institutionalizing American literature.

As English courses proliferated at the turn of the twentieth century, textbooks, usually compiled by professors, appeared to service the emergent academic market.[13] Such texts surveyed American writing but produced little or no consensus about the relative worth and ranking of native authors. In fact, no recognized canon of American literature existed at the time of the subdiscipline's academic formation or, indeed, during Howells's lifetime. Although, as Shumway argues, a few "standard authors" were recognized, "nothing united these authors as distinctively American." Given the predomination of British over American literature in nascent departments of English, it is not surprising, moreover, "that the American literature canon would emerge slowly, at the margins of the field, during the late 1920s and 1930s, and that it would be sometime during the next decade before that process was ratified and recognized."[14]

Howells's own roster of "standard authors" coincided, by and large, with those in contemporaneous textbooks, which credited half a dozen New England writers with laying the foundation of American literature. These were Emerson, Hawthorne, Holmes, Longfellow, Lowell, and Whittier—with Fuller, Stowe, and Thoreau sometimes added as satellites. Irving, Cooper, and Bryant were seen to have constituted an earlier group, centered on New York City, but the New Yorkers were customarily subordinated to the New Englanders. As Nina Baym points out, the "standard authors" were often figured "as quasi-allegorical personifications of some aspect of what . . . was called the New England mind. The basic scheme installed Whittier as the Reformer, Longfellow as the Poet, Holmes as the Wit, Lowell as Man of Letters, Emerson as Teacher or Philosopher . . . and Hawthorne as Artist."[15] At different stages of his career Howells might reasonably have laid claim to one or another of these roles (except, perhaps, Emerson's), but it was mainly to Lowell's place that The Dean of American Letters succeeded.

When The Dean spoke ex cathedra, however, it was not from Lowell's Smith Chair but from the "Editor's Easy Chair." Between December 1900 and April 1920, the month before he died, not a single month elapsed without the appearance of Howells's department in *Harper's Monthly,* which along with his 233 consecutive columns also published most of his fiction, poetry, memoirs, and travel writing. Aside from the *Monthly* and the other Harper magazines (*Harper's Weekly, Harper's Bazar,* the *North American Review*), Howells's access to public visibility was chiefly through the press. Both as an object of literary gossip and as a subject of interviews, The Dean was considered newsworthy.

II

"CURSED BE the writer who first allowed a journalist to reproduce his remarks freely!" proclaims Milan Kundera. "He started the process that can only lead to the disappearance of the writer: he who is responsible for every one of his words." Kundera means that the interviewer displaces and erases the writer-subject by asking only questions "of interest to him, of no interest to you," by using only the responses "that suit him," and by translating your words "into his own vocabulary, his own manner of thought."[16]

Howells was not the guilty first party to an interview, but he was certainly present at the birth of this journalistic genre after the Civil War,[17] and he soon became accustomed to the vagaries of paragraphers. He told his sister in 1895 about stopping "to look at an opossum before our butcher's door on the Avenue." When he had asked the butcher's boy who would buy such unusual fare, "He said colored people, and he showed me how fat it was." An eavesdropping reporter was hovering nearby, and the next day's *Herald* carried the amazing scoop: " 'Mr. Howells is fond of opossum,' etc." If he were not "a tolerably unconscious person," Howells added, "I should feel myself watched at every turn." In the same letter he debunked a recent story about his intrepidly slaying a bat during an after-dinner speech. In fact, a young Irishman had dispatched the winged intruder, but the reporters present "decided that the most could be got out of the fake that I killed it."[18]

The fakery of interviews is dramatized in the opening chapter of *The Rise of Silas Lapham,* in which the devious Bartley Hubbard elicits the Paint King's braggadocio, all the better to skewer him in the "Solid Men of Boston" series. Howells himself had been victimized by a concocted interview in 1880, which nearly stirred up trouble with his former *Atlantic* superior, James T. Fields.[19] Once he began to give real interviews in 1883, however, Howells gave them frequently, and he became "a particularly responsive subject."[20] Unlike Lapham, Howells was no pushover for pushy reporters. On the contrary, as one of them marveled, "Mr. Howells by no means permits his visitor to put all the questions." Adept himself at the "gentle inquisitorial art," The Dean easily switched roles, giving interviewers a dose of their own medicine: "He hardly finishes replying to one inquiry before he puts another, and such a probing one that again one feels himself being turned into 'copy' or splashed out into a bit of 'color.' "[21]

Aside from Mark Twain, on whom the New York papers often relied for colorful copy, Howells may have been the most quoted writer in America during his last twenty years. When he jestingly beseeched Clemens for an interview in 1901, he was speaking from his own extensive experience:

> I have long been an admirer of your complete works, several of which I have read, and I am with you shoulder to shoulder in the cause of foreign missions. I would respectfully request a personal interview, and if you will appoint some day and hour most inconvenient to you, I will call at your baronial hall. I cannot doubt from the account of your courtesy given me by the Twelve Apostles, who once visited you in your Hartford home and were mistaken for a sindicate of lightning rod men, that our meeting will be mutually agreeable.[22]

Interviews may have been disagreeable, but they were essential to the creation of The Dean, by propagating belief in an archetypal, rags-to-riches fable of Howells's career. "Americans felt sure of the national cultural achievement in his art and in him as its avatar," Edwin H. Cady observes. "They could enjoy wholeheartedly his being the first received American artist to tell the story of the development of his mind."[23] The alteration of Howells's public image during the 1890s is reflected in interviews by two members of the rising literary generation.

In 1894, Stephen Crane published in the *New York Times* a brief but evocative account of "An Interesting Talk with William Dean Howells." Also titled "Fears Realists Must Wait," the piece focused on the apprehension shared by both writers that a reactionary wave of romantic best-sellers had recently engulfed realism. Howells, in Crane's eyes, is the champion of serious, but not importunately didactic, fiction:

> "When a writer desires to preach in an obvious way he should announce his intention—let him cry out then that he is in the pulpit. But it is the business of the novel—"

> "Ah!" said the other man.
>
> "It is the business of the novel to picture the daily life in the most exact terms possible, with an absolute and clear sense of proportion. That is the important matter —the proportion."

Crane's Howells is recognizable as the embattled polemicist of the "Editor's Study," still launching squibs against literary miscreants. Writing merely to amuse people, he avers, is "altogether vulgar": "The author is a sort of trained bear, if you accept certain standards. If literary men are to be the public fools, let us at any rate have it clearly understood, so that those of us who feel differently can take measures."[24]

By contrast, Theodore Dreiser's far mellower Howells is recognizable as the avuncular Dean. There were two Dreiser interviews, ostensibly, although the first was almost certainly a fabrication. Ulrich Halfmann thinks that Dreiser never spoke to Howells at all in 1898, basing this "interview" instead on a questionnaire to which Howells briefly responded, and "a collage of unacknowledged quotations and paraphrases" from *My Literary Passions* (1895), skillfully "arranged as 'answers' to imaginary questions."[25] The plagiarized piece, first published in *Success* in April 1898, attained wide circulation through reprintings; and it went far toward identifying Howells with the Gospel of Wealth, whose bootstrap uplift realized the American Dream. "How He Climbed Fame's Ladder," ran the title: "William Dean Howells Tells the Story of His Long Struggle for Success, and His Ultimate Triumph. . . A poor Ohio Printer Boy who Became a Great Novelist." Dreiser begins by asking the "famous novelist" for his opinion about "what constitutes success in life"—whether, indeed, he is a proponent of "the belief that everything is open to the beginner who has sufficient energy and perseverance." "Add brains," Howells is said to have said with a smile, "and I will agree."[26]

The second Dreiser interview, which apparently *did* take place, was published in *Ainslee's* in March 1900.[27] Here "The Real Howells" is presented as "one of the noblemen of literature," a personage even "greater than his literary volumes make him out to be." It is in this piece, in fact, that Dreiser dubbed Howells "the Dean of American Letters"—the earliest such usage I have found in a national magazine.[28] The context was praise for Howells as a literary patron, one who agreed to read an unknown western writer's novel merely on Dreiser's recommendation.

> I was rather astonished at the liberal offer, and thanked him for the absent one. It was no idle favor of conversation, either. The book was forwarded, and, true to his word, he read it, doing what he could to make the merit of the work a source of reward for the author. There were several similar instances within a comparatively short period, and I heard of others from time to time until it all became impressively plain—how truly generous and humane is the Dean of American Letters. The great literary philanthropist, I call him.[29]

Howells's private generosity is construed by Dreiser as public-minded philanthropy. As the Dean of American Letters, Howells becomes virtually indistinguishable from, say, Andrew Carnegie (at whose table he sometimes sat):[30] the one building literary reputations as the other builds libraries to hold all the resulting books. The difference between Crane's Howells and Dreiser's Howells is the difference between the modest mentor and the monumentalized benefactor. It was the latter, of course, who became an object of scorn for those, later including Dreiser himself, who were eager to shake the Victorian pillars.

II

HOWELLS'S EAGLE eye for good new work and his genius for fostering young writers have been often remarked upon and justly praised. Ellen Moers, for one, asserts that "other literary men in other times and places have attained Howells's position of leadership in the world of letters, but surely none ever discharged its obligations more gracefully and more generously on behalf of youthful talent."[31] Cady, for another, commends Howells's nurturance of such realistic camp followers as Harold Frederic, Stephen Crane, and Frank Norris. "Full coverage of Howells's relations with the rising young men and women writers of his age would fill a large book in itself," Cady says.[32] Although no one has yet undertaken such a book, specific studies do exist of Howells's dealings with Charles W. Chesnutt and Charlotte Perkins Gilman.[33]

One of the vicissitudes of Howells's career was that the generosity of "the great literary philanthropist" was so poorly repaid by his beneficiaries. Of course, many of them, including those who might most ably have defended The Dean from the venomous moderns, did not live to give Howells proper credit. Among these who died before their time and his were Frederic (1898), Crane (1900), and Norris (1902), as well as H. H. Boyesen (1895), Paul Laurence Dunbar (1906), Clyde Fitch (1909) and Sarah Orne Jewett (1909). Jewett's career had been abridged by injury and illness some years before her death, and Chesnutt was effectively silenced by his refusal to meet mainstream expectations for "race fiction." Other protégés, such as Hamlin Garland and Henry Blake Fuller, early abandoned the realist cause.

In two important instances, however, the fault lay with Howells himself for not winning the allegiance of younger writers who were among his strongest natural allies. Howells's critical acumen was so unusually sharp that it is easy to forget he made some serious misjudgments. With Theodore Dreiser and Edith Wharton, his lack of appreciation ultimately damaged his own literary reputation. To grasp the full significance of Howells's failures with Dreiser and Wharton, it is useful to consider an incident involving Robert Herrick, a writer with Yankee roots whose Chicago novels had impressed Howells, who was particularly alert to midwestern newcomers.

The purest survival of The Age of Howells may, in fact, have been Herrick, who dared to take on the moderns with the same ferocity with which Howells had once challenged the romanticists—except that whereas Howells had rallied his own generation (and the next) against an entrenched literary past, Herrick railed against his younger contemporaries in defense of a Howellsian cause that was now superannuated. In 1929 Herrick denounced Hemingway and other peddlers of "filth" in the *Bookman*, a magazine founded in the 1890s that was showing its age by the 1920s. "What Is Dirt?" Herrick asked, finding the answer in the noisome lewdness of *A Farewell to Arms*, which was "mere garbage" that smelled, as he alliteratively added in another attack, of the "boudoir, the brothel, and the bar."[34]

There is rich irony here; it was the apparent moral vagrancy of Herrick's own early novel, *Together* (1908), that once had alarmed his erstwhile mentor. It would be so easy to caricature Howells's reaction to *Together*—as the very sort of Victorian prudery for which The Dean was later lambasted—that it is necessary to quote in full his 1909 letter to Herrick, as a prime example of Howells's close and subtle moral reasoning. The point of the letter was for Howells as potential reviewer to forewarn Herrick of qualms about the novel and to give him a chance, off the record, either to dispel them or else to bid Howells keep silent.

> I have been reading your books with great interest, and I am ready to write of them. But before I do so, I think I ought to tell you that I must express a very mixed mind about the last of them [*Together*]. There are two ways of looking at it: I can regard it as simply a picture of certain sides of American life, usually blinked, by an impartial observer whose sole business was to get them to the reader's knowledge; or I may regard it as in some sort a polemic for wider freedom in the sexual relations than the accepted ethics now grant. The episode of Margaret Pole and her lover, who go off several days together, and wreak their love for each other, with no after compunction, has especially given me question. If you have portrayed it as a thing that happens, and stand quite outside of it morally, you are within your rights as an artist; but if you mean that it was a thing to have done without shame or without sin, you put yourself [in] a position which the criticism deriving from such ethics as the world knows may and must question. In a measure this is the case with the whole book, and its several potential or actual adulteries.
>
> I am the more confused because the reading of the story has not impaired my sense of your power as it comes from a serious and conscientious mind, or my respect for your literary quality. If I bring you to book it is not with bell and candle. If you wish to straighten me out with some word which the story does not speak, this is the moment. Or if you would rather on the whole that I should not write of your books I shall not misunderstand you, or depreciate you. (*SL*, 5:267)

It is important to note that Howells's objection was not simply to the portrayal of sex per se, or even of adulterous sex, but rather to the moral tone of the surrounding narrative. The artist has the perogative, he allows, of showing the most salacious reality, as long as that representation goes, as it were, without comment: offered with strict and scientific neutrality as "a thing that happens." (Howells may well have been thinking here of Zola, in defense of whose artistic rights he himself had incurred considerable abuse.) But Herrick's imagination, Howells senses, has subtly endorsed what offends common decency (the constituency of Howellsian realism) and thus has taken a position that "the criticism deriving from such ethics as the world knows may and must question." It is conscious or unconscious *im*morality (not objective *a*morality, which stands "quite outside") that the Howellsian critic must protest. The artistry of the *im*moral writer must ultimately be judged defective insofar as it fails to register the reality of accepted ethics reacting against "a thing that happens."

Herrick staunchly defended his work, insisting that he had "NEVER written polemically" and, certainly, had "never for one moment intended to hold a brief for free love." As for Margaret Pole and her lover, this was another example in the novel of "extreme individualism, which is the politely philosophical term we give to selfishness." For *these* adulterers, however, "this fulfillment of self at the cost of moral law, was FOR THE TIME an actual gain, a real enoblement." However much we may deplore adultery, he argued, "it is only right to realize that there is actual gain up to a certain point of spiritual life for some cases in sin" (*SL*, 5:267–68 n).

Such a contention tested the limits of Howells's tolerance by affronting his notion of accepted ethics. But Herrick's challenge to Howellsian realism was no greater, after all, than the distinctive deviations of Frederic, Crane, and Norris; and despite his reservations, Howells remained flexible enough to embrace them all, even as he made his differences from them known. Howells did not hesitate, therefore, to commend Herrick's work to Brander Matthews. While suggesting that in *Together* "the eternal femininity which always more or less bedevils him, really seems to make wreck of a good puritanic morality," Howells concluded, "Still it is a great book, and some of the earlier ones are greater" (*SL*, 5:269). In his review Howells reiterated his private differences with Herrick, chastising him for an indulgent disposition toward Margaret Pole's adultery, and complaining that he exaggerates the degree of feminine discontent within modern marriage. But these forthright criticisms were heavily outweighed in the review by praise for Herrick as one of the very few "American novelists of a later generation than Mr. Henry James, who are at once moralists and artists, who set the novel of manners above all other fiction, and who aim at excellence in it with unfailing conscience." Even where Herrick delineates "emotion and behavior long blinked in Anglo-Saxon fiction" with more frankness "than we once supposed desirable" for young women, Howells credits him with recognizing the painful facts "with a pathological decency."[35]

At the time of this review in 1909, Howells's critical voice had become indivisible from his Deanly authority—to the point where one might perceive in his dealings with Herrick some potential or actual abuse of power. The entire episode could be interpreted, from this angle, as an example of The Dean's censorial intimidation. By preemptorily calling Herrick on the carpet, was not Howells practicing a kind of extortion? Threatening, albeit implicitly, to withhold approval from a less established writer much in need of his support? "If I bring you to book it is not with bell and candle," wrote Howells, nicely turning a phrase. But the Deanly power to cast out demons went unquestioned in his decision not to exorcize Herrick in particular. Herrick undoubtedly felt stigmatized, if not demonized, by The Dean's disapproval. He was certainly quick to refute any imputation that he had joined the devil's party in *Together.*

It would be difficult to sustain such an unrelievedly inimical reading of the exchange, however. Howells's disagreements with Herrick were neither heavy-handed nor underhanded; and when Herrick failed to mollify Howells in private, The Dean published his review anyway, granting far more space to praise than to condemnation. In the context of some other, far more outraged, reviews of *Together,* Howells's objections were relatively mild.

There is inevitably something ominous, however, about the concentration of power. Howells presented, as Cady says, "an extraordinary figure to the young men as model, as mentor, and as father-image to emulate or rebel against. The one certain thing was that they could not ignore him" (p. 208). What's ominous is that The Dean could certainly ignore *them*—and "them" included not only his "Anglo-Saxon" Oedipal sons, but also male writers who were racially other, as well as the many female writers for whom he represented a very different "father-image," one inseparable from the patriarchal order of the publishing establishment.

Under the circumstances of the modern literary marketplace, in which there was no such thing as bad publicity, the fullest measure of Deanly power lay precisely in Howells's discretion not to exercise it. The deepest cut of all was for The Dean *not* to speak ex cathedra about a promising writer. Cady asserts that Howells had no desire "to make little Howellses out of the young":

> All he wanted from them was full and honest work, and he would tolerate any amount of variance from his notions, even defiance of them, so long as he thought true work was forthcoming. He saw no reason to muffle his own convictions when a serious young writer flouted them. But he did not retaliate, either. The furthest length he would go, and that in the face of what seemed to him extreme provocation, was to withhold his reputation-making word. (pp. 209–10)

But this extreme possibility, as Cady himself observes, is quietly broached in the letter to Herrick, when Howells suggests—as if it were entirely *Herrick's* choice—that if he should not write any review, he would "not misunderstand you, or depreciate you." Whether Howells fully realized it or not, his critical silence, far more than his public disapproval, threatened to "depreciate" a writer's stock.

III

NO ONE FELT this fact more keenly than Dreiser, the only one of The Dean's literary heirs to write a Great American Novel along Howellsian lines: *An American Tragedy* (1925). When Dreiser first met Howells (if, indeed, they *ever* did meet) he felt envious, as Moers says, "of those who had achieved success and suspicious of the power of the critic to award it."[36] But Howells disarmed the aspirant—who had arrived "longing, verses in hand, for recognition"—by freely offering to read his poems. "He is not a rich man and must work for his living," Dreiser observed, with characteristic attention to economic considerations, "yet he will take of his time to read the struggler's material and recommend him according to his merit."[37] Howells, in other words, was accustomed to giving away his valuable time; and in Dreiser's case, as the young writer bragged to his friends, The Dean had expressed such a "hearty liking" for his verse that the poet was encouraged to believe book publication was possible.[38]

At the outset, Dreiser's devotion to Howells was so intense that he sent him a kind of literary love letter in response to an 1902 "Easy Chair" essay on Longfellow. It was a bizarre and faintly suicidal letter, in fact, written in the throes of Dreiser's nervous collapse after the failure of *Sister Carrie* (1900); and it reflected its author's mental disturbance. Dreiser took up Howells's reflection about Longfellow that "They who fall become the closer friends to those who remain untouched, and as everything is dearer since it dies, all memories of such as have lived and labored within touch of us take the twinge of a personal grief, and we know too late how much they were to us who can be nothing more." He has been so affected by this "mellow, kindly and withal so lonely" sentiment, Dreiser declares, that he has hastened to offer "a word of fellow feeling and appreciation ere the 'next round' take you and it be too late."

Dreiser goes on to express his deep "spiritual affection" for Howells, as well as his admiration for some of his recent poems, to which he has clung in moments of despair "when I can no longer feign to believe that life has either a purpose or a plan." The work of Hardy and Tolstoy has also afforded consolation, and Dreiser has to wonder if Howells's "expressed estimate of Hardy" has really been adequate: "I had rather hoped to find an acknowledgement of the soul of the Englishman, equal to that of the Russian—a chain of spiritual sympathy binding you together." But Dreiser is not writing to quibble: "The beauty of your mental attitude is enough for me." And he professes, in a murky concluding paragraph, that the prospect of returning "to the dust" does not disturb him if "the common ground is to be credited with the flowering out of such minds as yours." The mystery of life itself will become clear: "Buried Howells and Hardys and Tolstoys shall explain it for me."[39]

Howells showed this letter to his sister, remarking that the ardor of "the writer who wishes to honor me while I am still above ground has its comic aspect; but I must not recognize it in my answer" (*SL,* 5:27). Unaware of Howells's true reaction, Moers speculates that the Dreiser letter, "with its pretentiousness, its arrogance and, worst, its unsuccessful imitation of some of the least attractive rhetorical flourishes of Howells's own style, must have annoyed Howells."[40] But if he was annoyed—as he might have been, for example, by Dreiser's praise of the poetry rather than the fiction, or by his nitpicking over Howells's treatment of Hardy—he did not show it.[41]

In fact, Howells was so deaf to the dolorous aggression in Dreiser's tone that he read a benign intent even in the letter's funereal preoccupations, which might easily have been taken otherwise, as inchoately expressing the idea that Dreiser had come to bury Howells, not to praise him. When one knows that Dreiser had to break through the wall of his own mute depression in order to write this letter (the only one extant from 1902 and perhaps the only one he wrote that grim year), it is easier to see it as a desperately conflicted act of literary affiliation in which Dreiser cleaves to/from Howells, wishing him well while wishing him dead. For Howells to find comedy here was inadvertently cruel, and his insensitivity to Dreiser may have carried into the reply he undoubtedly sent (but that does not survive).

The 1902 letter seems to point backward to the matter of *Sister Carrie.* In his *Ainslee's* interview, Dreiser had explicitly mentioned Howells's indispensable support of Crane and Abraham Cahan: "He has, time after time, praised so liberally that paragraphers love to speak of him as the 'lookout on the watch tower,' straining for a first glimpse of approaching genius."[42] From the interviewer's point of view, the lookout had not very far to look; Dreiser must have hoped soon to bask in Howells's recognition of his own first novel, to enjoy the same vindication bestowed on other faithful disciples.

It never happened. Instead of becoming Dreiser's partisan against Doubleday, Page and Company, his repressively uncomprehending publisher, The Dean maintained a withering silence, not bothering even to negotiate the terms of his disapproval, as he later would with Herrick. For whatever reason, Howells simply could not or would not abide Dreiser as one of his literary sons.[43] When they ran into each other at the *Harper's Monthly* office, Howells allegedly told him, "You know, I don't like *Sister Carrie,*" and walked on.[44]

After his 1902 letter, Dreiser seems not to have approached Howells again, and his "spiritual affection" waned. On Howells's side the silence became nearly absolute[45] until 1920, when he included "The Lost Phoebe" in *The Great Modern American Stories* and said a few perfunctory words about Dreiser in the introduction. Any residual loyalty in Dreiser must have vanished during the fracas over

The "Genius" in 1916, when Howells was conspicuously absent from the broad ranks of those united in defense of Dreiser's artistic freedom. It was as if the situation of the Haymarket case had been reversed: this time Howells was nearly alone in his *refusal* to inveigh against a perceived injustice.[46] Along with Agnes Repplier and Ellen Glasgow, he took the position that he would not lend his name against suppression of *The "Genius"* without reading it first.

It is understandable that Dreiser did nothing to allay the ritual slaughter of Howells's reputation during the 1920s and that he later abetted his partisan first biographer's supercilious ignorance. "I suppose Howells was a writer," opined Dorothy Dudley. "I am a reader who will never know. Try as I will, I can't read him, neither his Easy Chair for Harper's Magazine, nor his endless novels. He wrote for the gentry of his times, and must have put to sleep the more restless members." " 'Yes, I know his books are pewky and damn-fool enough,' " Dreiser agreed—although he did go on to defend his somewhat unaccountable admiration for *Their Wedding Journey*.[47]

The same dismissive tone was struck by Edith Wharton in 1916, in a letter to her protégé Gaillard Lapsley, who had proffered some feeble excuse for failing to visit her. "I do feel, you know," Wharton archly replied, "that your reasons for *not* coming to see me are a little like those which prevent the elderly married couple in a Howells novel of 450 pages from telling the young girl in their charge that they have heard that the young man who is 'attentive' to her once drove another girl to a quilting party."[48] Wharton's cultivated disdain for Howells might well have been avoidable had he ever taken her as seriously as she deserved. All things considered, R. W. B. Lewis suggests, Howells "was probably Edith Wharton's closest predecessor in American literary history." If, near the beginning of her career, she had read his famous account in *Literary Friends and Acquaintance* about the laying on of hands, "she must, in 1903, have felt herself to stand in the same honorable line of succession."[49] By 1903, however, Howells had largely written her off.

Their relationship went back to 1880, when Longfellow had pressed Wharton's adolescent poems upon Howells, as editor of the *Atlantic,* and he had selected one of them for publication. Twenty years later, after Howells became a talent scout for Harper and Brothers, Wharton was one among several up-and-coming writers he approached in that capacity, asking for submissions. He had been quietly following her career as a fiction writer, he told her, and now he was glad to have the opportunity of expressing "your old editor's—perhaps your first editor's?—very great pleasure" in her work. Might she have some fiction to show? "Of course a novel is preferred and expected; but a book of any sort would be gladly considered; if it happened to be a story of contemporary American life, with no hint of history in it—not of day before yesterday—that would be most to my mind" (*SL,* 4:252–53).

Wharton's first novel *The Valley of Decision* (1901), steeped as it was in the day before yesterday, was definitely *not* what Howells had in mind. "I have not read the book yet," he later confessed to Norton, who greatly admired its mastery of Italian history. Howells was "dreading somewhat to find Stendhal in it as I find James in her stories. She is a great creature, and I wish she used her own voice solely" (*SL*, 5:29).[50] He never did read the novel; if he had, he might have seen it as yet another unfortunate defection to the enemy camp of historical romance.

Along with seven other books, Wharton's *Crucial Instances* received brief notice in the "Easy Chair" for October 1901; but when S. Weir Mitchell recommended *The House of Mirth* in 1905, Howells admitted he had not "read anything of Mrs. Wharton's except her short stories, merely because I have not come in the way of her books." This excuse was as lame as his resolution: "But I shall yet read them." Howells's reluctance, as before, stemmed from a sense of Wharton's fiction as derivative. "I think it a pity she should have remained so long in the bondage of James," he told Mitchell, "for she is [a] great enough spirit to be free and to be herself" (*SL*, 5:143–44). Thus while nearly all of Wharton's major novels appeared during Howells's lifetime, he remained steadfastly ignorant of her achievement, having given her up just at the point where she *had* found her own voice, in writing stories of contemporary American life. As with Dreiser, Howells failed to recognize both the originality of Wharton's work and its continuity with his own, subjecting her to a critical silence that, coming from The Dean, effectively depreciated her literary worth.

All the while, Howells gladly cooperated with Wharton on projects she initiated in behalf of their friend in common, Henry James—such as her unsuccessful campaign in 1911 to convince the Swedish Academy to award him the Nobel Prize. But he drew the line two years later, when Wharton confidentially solicited American contributions for a $5,000 seventieth-birthday gift, to match a similar offering from James's English friends. Wharton presumptuously counted on Howells's support, hastily drafting a letter in both their names, later to be cosigned by him, she expected. Although, as she told Barrett Wendell, it would have been better to collect eight or ten sponsoring signatures, there was time to obtain only one; and it was well understood why it had to be Howells's: not only was he James's "very old & close friend," he was also "the doyen of American letters."[51]

The Dean/Doyen balked, however, as soon as he got wind of the scheme, believing that James would be mortified by any such monetary tribute. Indeed, when James was let in on the secret, he "lost his head completely" and furiously demanded an end to the whole business. "What a mercy that scandalous attempt on poor James's delicacy was so promptly defeated!" Howells exclaimed to Lilla Perry. "I look back on it with horror, blessing God that I had no part in it" (*SL*, 6:33).

In the end it was Wharton who was mortified by James's vexation—"I can never get over this," she wailed to Lapsley—and she blamed Howells for her troubles. "It was apparently Mr Howells," she wrote to Sara Norton, "who betrayed our confidence, & revealed the plan to Mrs Wm James, who cabled to H. J. that I was 'raising a fund' for his support—apparently giving him the impression that I was collecting money to pay his debts or buy him an annuity!"[52] Howells was not, in fact, the one who tipped off James; but Wharton's wrath was as severe as her embarrassment, and she fulminated about the "ineffable letter" she had received from Howells: "senile and querulous—*how* it explains his novels!"[53]

By 1920, when Howells proposed to put "The Mission of Jane" into *The Great Modern American Stories,* Wharton was long past her pique; and she responded fondly and graciously, thanking him for his editorial kindness so many years ago to the "very shy young woman" who had sent him "a handful of worthless verse." "She is very glad to think that any work of hers . . . may have partly liquidated her debt," Wharton added. She was "especially proud that you should think she comes under the rubric of 'best' " (*SL,* 6:136 n).

For Howells's benefit in this letter, Wharton played a polite parody of the timid girl she once had been: the "she" who gracefully bows to her elder. But Wharton was now the experienced and unsubmissive woman who was soon to publish the masterful *Age of Innocence* (1920), and she must have wondered about Howells's selection for his anthology. Why choose so early and so relatively trifling a story—from *The Descent of Man* (1904)—when so many better ones were available? Perhaps she suspected the shallowness of Howells's knowledge of her work.

Nonetheless when Sinclair Lewis savaged Howells in his Nobel Prize address in 1930, Wharton came gallantly to his defense. Her only quarrel with the speech, she privately told Lewis, was "that you should have made it the occasion of saying anything depreciatory of Howells," who despite his inevitable limitations had painted "the first honestly realistic picture of the American mediocracy." Along with Robert Grant's *Unleavened Bread* (1900), *A Modern Instance* had really paved the way for *Main Street*—not to mention (she didn't) *The Custom of the Country* (1913), arguably Wharton's greatest novel. She admonished Lewis to reread some of Howells's best fiction; she was confident he then would wish "to unsay what you said of him."[54] It is unlikely that Lewis took this advice, and Wharton herself was soon to unsay what *she* had said, when she publicly reconsidered Howells in *A Backward Glance* (1934) and reverted to her exasperation soon after the James fiasco. Now she perceived only "moral timidity" in *A Modern Instance,* which rendered it inferior to *Unleavened Bread* and left Grant "the first in the field which he was eventually to share with Lewis and Dreiser."[55]

Dreiser, counted here and elsewhere by 1934 as a weighty presence in American writing, might well have savored The Dean's displacement in Wharton's eyes by so slight a figure as Robert Grant—who at least had read Wharton's novels, if not Dreiser's, appreciatively! This turn of events would have seemed impossible either to Dreiser or to Wharton in their youth a generation earlier. But Howells himself, sharply aware of his fading powers, had early sensed his vulnerability to such a crushing deflation. In 1903, reading what struck him as the absurdly self-important autobiographies of Richard Henry Stoddard and John T. Trowbridge, he pondered "their contrasting unimportance" beside Mark Twain (whose biography he had recently been urged to write) and applied the lesson in humility to himself. "I think I will write my own life," he told Thomas Sergeant Perry, "but these other minor authors have taught me that if I am to make a worth-while book, I must tell of what I have been in the love of literature, rather than of what I have done. The way they whoop it up over their forgotten books, T. especially, is amusing" (*SL,* 5:68). If nothing else, Howells wished not to become "amusing" the same way as Trowbridge; and so he tried to avoid putting on airs.

As a result, there was a discrepancy between The Dean's imposing public image and Howells's modest placement of himself among the "minor authors" of his day. As he was living, after all, in The Age of Howells, it was difficult to know sometimes just *who* he was. "I should not mind being old, so much," he confided to Thomas Bailey Aldrich, "if I always had the young, sure grip of myself. What I hate is this dreamy fumbling about my own identity, in which I detect myself at odd times. It seems sometimes as if it were somebody else, and I sometimes wish it were" (*SL,* 5:32). Soon after taking his seat in the "Easy Chair," in order to distinguish his job from that of Henry Mills Alden, the editor really in charge of *Harper's Monthly,* Howells began referring to himself (in a pun that captured his occasionally fumbling sense of self) as the "Unreal Editor."

IV

FINANCIALLY SECURE after 1900, thanks to his exclusive contract with Harper and Brothers, Howells set about earning his keep, worried by signs of his waning popularity. There was, first, the unwelcoming reception of *The Kentons:* not only its failure to attain serial publication and its poor sales, but also the tepid and even hostile reviews. The worst blow was the excoriation of Howells in the *Atlantic Monthly,* the magazine with which he once had been synonymous. To Harriet W. Preston, who lifted her nose and raised her skirts against Howells's odiously commonplace Ohioan characters, the dreary adult Kentons were outdone only by "their vastly inferior offspring" and "the repulsive Bittridge," adjudged a fitting mate for Grant's vampish Selma in *Unleavened Bread.* Preston had to doubt the propriety, if not the decency, "of giving such types the publicity of print at all"—types that seemed to conjure up for her some incestuous eugenic nightmare on the order of the degenerate Jukes clan. "They are the scum and spawn of a yeasty deep,—the monstrous offspring of barbarous and illicit social relations. They are necessarily short-lived, and, it is to be hoped, sterile." To have removed such deformities from the sideshow where they belong and foisted them on the public in a novel "is like riding in pink, and with winding of horns, to a hunt of cockroaches!"[56]

In the face of such aggressive stupidity Howells was helpless to act when Bliss Perry sent him the manuscript and later the proofs of Preston's screed, obviously hoping The Dean would manage to lift this cross from his own editorial shoulders (or at least understand that Perry himself had no wish to give offense). Howells's integrity required him to put it all back on the editor and reviewer: "If you are satisfied to print and she to write such a criticism, it is certainly not for me, on any account whatever, to interpose an objection" (*SL,* 5:39). He could not permit even the appearance of his suppressing criticism, as he acidulously told Perry, "which you thought could not possibly offend me, although you submitted it to my censure for everything or anything annoying in it." He had never sought to control reviews of his work, and he was not about to start (*SL,* 5:39 n).

Although Howells appeared to brush off such unpleasantries, they tinged his private estimation of his fiction. If he could not suppress bad reviews, he would withdraw his work when he doubted its merits and feared for its reception. While writing *Letters Home* (1903), his follow-up to *The Kentons,* Howells told Aldrich that he was "very much in love with it at first, and not so much now" and that he intended "to serialize it anonymously" (*SL,* 5:11). This wish was not granted, and Howells remained unhappy with the novel, which he had whittled down from an ambitious "study of manners and contemporary events" into something more narrowly psychological. "I wish I had had time and nerve to carry out my original plan," he rued, in the same letter in which he amused his sister with Dreiser's fulsome funereal bouquet (*SL,* 5:27). Howells later concluded that the epistolary form had been "a mistake," and he told Aurelia that his "ill-imagined story in letters" was "a failure": "like all old people I have begun to repeat myself" (*SL,* 5:28 n).

Despite Howells's misgivings, *Letters Home* was, in fact, a small but sprightly novel with much to recommend it.[57] But it "shivered about without a friend" after publication (*SL* 5:79), perhaps because the inapt title hurt sales. So Harper and Brothers wanted Howells to believe: "In this sophisticated age, people do not want letters nor homes, it seems. These things are very droll, but I incline to think the publishers are half right about the matter" (*SL,* 5:69). Howells could not, in any event, risk two weak outings in a row; and so he arranged to postpone the appearance of *Miss Bellard's Inspiration* (1905), finished late in 1903, until after the serial run and book publication of *The Son of Royal Langbrith* (1904), the only novel completed during this decade that evinced the vigor and amplitude of his finest work. "I think it would be a mistake," Howells explained to his editor, Frederick A. Duneka,[58] "to follow a failure like 'Letters Home' with a story like the present, and that their joint effect would be injurious to the North American story, which is a novel of some psychological importance" (*SL,* 5:76). The strategy seemed to work; *Langbrith,* carried by good reviews, was reprinted twice within a year of publication, making it an encouraging exception to Howells's recent doldrums in the marketplace.

Like *The Kentons, Miss Bellard's Inspiration* never appeared in serial; like *Letters Home,* it was damned with faint praise and then it languished in the bookstores. As for Howells's English travel books, the outcome of his trip abroad in 1904 to accept his honorary degree from Oxford, neither *London Films* (1905) nor *Certain Delightful English Towns* (1906) was "selling delightfully" (*SL,* 5:195); when Harper and Brothers actually took a loss, Howells urgently proposed a discounted tourist edition of *London Films* as a way to recoup. (The publishers ignored him.)

Howells's problems late in his career are epitomized by his struggle with "The Children of the Summer," a novel he had begun in the 1870s, laid aside at Elinor's request (she disapproved of its use of Shaker characters), and picked up again in 1907. As Howells straggled through the composition over the next two years, finding it hard to graft new growth onto old stock, he was convinced he had finally lost his touch. While reading proofs of the novel, he told Henry Blake Fuller in March 1909, "it came over me that it was past the time with me to write fiction. I had a kind of sickness of the job. . . . I should once never have believed that I could feel so" (*SL,* 5:271). Although the novel's publication had been announced as imminent, Howells begged Duneka to put it off until he could "give it a thorough overhauling—perhaps till next year" (*SL,* 5:271 n). But next year stretched into the next year, and even then, after the plates had already been cast, Howells could not bring himself to let the book go forth. He asked for another, indefinite postponement. Duneka reluctantly obliged, and "The Children of the Summer" appeared only posthumously as *The Vacation of the Kelwyns* (1920).

Independence Day in 1909, Howells wrote to his brother Joe about sorting through all his books in preparation for the Library Edition. This painful process ("like delving in the tombs") redoubled Howells's awareness of the irretrievability of his youth. "Things suggest themselves, but they don't grip me, and hold me to them as they used." He still hoped to catch his wind again, "but just now I am fagged, there's no denying it" (*SL,* 5:278–79). Dismayed by his diminishing energy and conscience-striken by his curtailed productivity, Howells had proposed a salary adjustment early in 1908, offering to take a cut on the pretext that Franklin Square had fallen on hard times following the Panic of 1907. Colonel Harvey, touched by the gesture, insisted that "the idea of making inroads upon your income had never occurred to me and I would not consent to do so in any circumstance, if for no other reason because I regard your present rumuneration wholly inadequate" (*SL,* 5:240 n).[59]

This was not mere chivalry on Harvey's part. In truth, Howells's publishers were happy enough to pay his generous salary whether his books sold or not; his value to them lay elsewhere. Cady suggests that Howells's role was shifting into a final phase: from The Dean to a "great Academician after the French fashion." As his writing "dwindled toward a suave but tired impressionism," Cady says, "and as his age and declining energies conspired with the deaths of more and more of his friends, he ceased gradually to be the leading man of letters or even the Dean of the faculty, and became a symbol of official culture."[60]

It was in this capacity that Howells repaid his publishers' investment. In a summary of his dealings with Franklin Square, prepared for use in J. Henry Harper's history of the firm, Howells testified to "the friendship which has always existed between my publishers and myself." Since 1900, he declared, "I have remained attached to the House of Harper & Brothers, with no desire for any other business relations." The admiration was completely mutual. Harvey would certainly have seconded Harper's official acknowledgment of their indebtedness to Howells "for his unswerving fidelity to their interests, and the constantly proven quality of his friendship, which has for many years now been one of their most cherished spiritual assets."[61] To be sure, Harvey, who had engaged Howells because "he wished me to belong to the shop," had a more tangibly material notion of assets than Harper, his predecessor at the helm; and he seized every opportunity to put Howells on display in the shop window. Thus in addition to sincere good will, a measure of calculated self-interest entered into the Colonel's orchestration of Howells's diamond jubilee. Toasting The Dean was simply good business, a means to good publicity for the company.

V

THE PARTY HARVEY sponsored for Howells's seventy-fifth birthday in 1912 recalled grand affairs from the glory days of the *Atlantic Monthly.* In fact, even before the *Atlantic* was organized, its future publisher had sponsored a "notable dinner" at the newly opened Parker House, with the New England clerisy in attendance: Emerson, Motley, Holmes, Longfellow, Lowell. Once the magazine was successfully launched, Lowell, the first editor, hosted several such gatherings, now including a few women. The first *Atlantic* event on the scale of a banquet occurred in December 1874, with editor Howells as master of ceremonies. Fond remembrance, by Holmes and others, was the order of the evening. Mark Twain, who barely qualified as a contributor—"A True Story" had just appeared in the November 1874 issue, and his "Old Times on the Mississippi" was to begin its serial run in January 1875—"was called upon to respond for 'The President of the United States and the Female Contributors of the *Atlantic.*'" Rising to the challenge, Mark Twain expressed his pleasant surprise that "the publishers before him acted in the present instance as though they really wanted to conciliate their menials," and he pronounced the dinner to be "quite as good as he would have had if he had stayed at home!"[62]

After the notorious Whittier Dinner two years later, when Mark Twain "*raised hell* about Emerson and Longfellow,"[63] he rather wished he *had* stayed home. Clemens was nevertheless invited back for the Autocrat's seventieth-birthday "breakfast" in 1879, when fully a third of the hundred guests were women. President Rutherford B. Hayes was among the dignitaries who could not attend, but he sent a congratulatory message.

The last of these occasions was an al fresco gala in honor of Harriet Beecher Stowe (who admitted to being "at least seventy") in 1882, twenty-five years after the founding of the *Atlantic.* Those present included all of its still living luminaries and the usual clutch of politicians and academics. Although the custom of commemorative literary dinners continued to prosper—Howells feasted his way through several decades and developed the girth to prove it—the *Atlantic* tradition, in which a prominent publisher joined with contributors for mutual acclamation, faded away until Colonel Harvey, with his flair for public relations, revived it.

Soon after the House of Harper was stabilized, Harvey "dressed up the eminent old lady with lipstick, a new hairdo, and fashionable clothes and began to present her properly in a long succession of luncheons and dinners."[64] Several of these affairs were ostensibly for the staff, but Harvey also invited reporters, who obligingly provided a splash of publicity. In 1902, when the American Booksellers' Association was feted at Franklin Square, *Harper's Weekly* carried a photograph; it became standard procedure for the house to promote itself in the *Weekly.* Harvey threw a stag party for Mark Twain, also in 1902, and then a much larger dinner three years later, in honor of Clemens's seventieth birthday. At this "sky-scraping banquet," as Howells called it, "172 immortals sat down to the best Delmonico could do, and remained glutting and guzzling food for reflection for five hours after the dinner was ended." The guest list impressed Howells as "the strangest mixture of literary celebrity and social notoriety that I have ever seen. The smart and the chic were both present, and not at separate tables, always" (*SL,* 5:138 and 140). President Theodore Roosevelt sent a letter. Howells read a "double-barreled" sonnet (twenty-eight lines), a form he invented for the occasion. Harvey, who presided, made certain that the affair received full coverage in a special supplement to *Harper's Weekly.*

The lavish Mark Twain Dinner and a similar celebration for Henry Mills Alden's seventieth birthday in 1906 were merely dress rehearsals for the Howells affair, a Babylonian extravaganza reminiscent of P. T. Barnum. "I hear it is to be the largest thing of the kind on record," Howells told his brother, "and I have begun to write out my few impromptu remarks."[65] Like the honoree's supposedly "impromptu" speech, there was nothing truly spontaneous about this occasion, and nothing was left to chance.[66] At half-past six on the evening of 2 March 1912, more than four hundred carefully chosen guests descended upon Sherry's, the poshest restaurant in New York, and "swarmed" (as Howells put it) "about a hundred tables on the floor" (*SL,* 6:16).[67] Among the assembled journalists, publishers, writers, and politicians was the president, *very* much in the flesh this time, in the corpulent person of William Howard Taft, a fellow Ohioan. The banquet had been moved to the day after Howells's actual birthday in order to accommodate the president's schedule; Harvey later boasted that "it was the first public dinner in New York that Taft had ever sat through."[68]

On a raised dais, like a trinity of Business, Art, and Politics, perched Colonel Harvey, with The Dean of American Letters at his right hand and the President of the United States at his left.[69] The Colonel opened the festivities with a greeting in which he cleverly interwove the titles of many Howells books ("your literary product"), generously mentioning even some that had appeared without the Harper imprint.

After a flattering introduction by Harvey, Taft paid homage to Howells with a syntactical creativity worthy of some later Republican presidents renowned for their fractured sentences: "I have traveled from Washington here to do honor to the greatest living American writer and novelist. I have done this because of the personal debt I feel for the pleasure he has given me in what he has written, in the pictures of American life and society and character he has painted, and with which I have had sufficient familiarity to know the truth and delicacy of his touch." Unlike Harvey, with his inventory of Howellsian titles, Taft neglected to mention exactly what he was "sufficiently familiar" with; he did, however, recall a simple act of kindness, received when Yale had awarded an honorary M.A. to Howells in 1881. That was the year of Taft's commencement, and as he nervously mounted the platform to receive his diploma, Howells had offered "some comforting words" to a young man he did not know and could not have expected to meet again. "That was more than thirty years ago," said the President, "but compliments don't wear out."

What followed were addresses from writers chosen by Harvey to represent the various literary arts in which Howells excelled. One spokesman was Winston Churchill, a lion of the best-seller list, with a string of romantic novels of the sort Howells detested—a writer The Dean had assiduously ignored and who had never before encountered Howells outside the pages of his books. Additional tribute was offered by Hamilton Wright Mabie, editor of the *Christian Union* and archreligionist, who once had denounced *The Rise of Silas Lapham* for its cold psychologism and dangerous agnosticism. Three obscurities of no known relationship to the guest of honor also held forth: Basil King, Augustus Thomas, and James Barnes. The only speaker with any ties to Howells was William Allen White, editor of the *Emporia Gazette,* who first had met him during his swing through Kansas in 1899. White had the temerity, on an occasion where the opulence of the feast was exceeded only by the luxuriance of the oratory, to praise Howells for his steadfast commitment to social justice.

Laudatory letters had been received beforehand from Arnold Bennett, Thomas Hardy, Arthur Pinero, James Barrie, H. G. Wells, and others in England, and also from unavoidably absent American colleagues, as well as a long and extraordinary tribute from Henry James, which he intended to be read at the dinner. But these and other missives instead were published in one or another of the Harper magazines. A similar spray of tributes from Mary Wilkins Freeman, Robert Herrick, W.E.B. Du Bois, and several more admirers was gathered by William Stanley Braithwaite in the *Boston Evening Transcript.*[70] Many private letters poured in; Howells needed weeks to acknowledge them all.

Howells appeared to take it all in stride as he rose to address the jubilant throng. The Dean glanced back over his long career, beginning with the summer day he had idled on the hill behind the Wayside with Hawthorne, who had told him, as if with prescience of the occasion at hand, "that there was nothing like recognition to make a man modest." Howells's modesty was certainly in evidence as he genuflected before the literary "stellar fires" he had known. He proudly called the roll:

> The list of them is very long, and I may say that if I missed the personal acquaintance of Cooper and Irving and Poe and Prescott I was personally acquainted with all the others in whom the story of American literature sums itself. I knew Hawthorne and Emerson and Walt Whitman; I knew Longfellow and Holmes and Whittier and Lowell; I knew Bryant and Bancroft and Motley; I knew Harriet Beecher Stowe and Julia Ward Howe; I knew Artemus Ward and Stockton and Mark Twain; I knew Parkman and Fiske. Names refulgent still, however the fire, never to be relumed, seems beginning to die out of some of them; names such as we have hardly the like of.

Anticipating an objection here, Howells declared that, in fact, "we have many like them, but of no more identity with them than they felt with one another." Speaking of himself as well as his literary friends and acquaintance, he added: "As far as they were truly great they must have perceived that they were not so great as they had grown to seem and each must have perceived even more clearly that the others were not so great."[71]

In his paper for the 1912 history of the House of Harper, Howells frankly acknowledged that "the long fight" for realism had been a losing one: "I perceive now that the monstrous rag-baby of romanticism is as firmly in the saddle as it was before the joust began, and that it always will be, as long as the children of men are childish."[72] But he used the occasion in his own honor to honor the realist movement: "A literature as authentic and distinctive as our journalism has grown up in the years since the Civil War . . . and with this literature as truly as with our commerce and our finance the American consciousness has increased."

In hoping for greater days yet to come, Howells stressed that the fundamental conditions now were different insofar as "all of human life has turned more and more to the light of democracy, the light of equality." This meant that literature, "which was once of the cloister, the school," has become "more and more of the forum and incidentally of the market-place." As a result, we no longer have "supremacies" or "primacies." "The gods, the half-gods, the heroes are gone, I hope not to return," Howells proclaimed, contravening Emerson; "and it is the high average which reigns in this as in all American things."[73]

As Heinz Ickstadt points out, Howells invoked the marketplace "with some hesitation," as if he "subconsciously distrusted the continuity between the forum and the market-place on which his whole argument rested." Working against the grain of the banquet, "which clearly celebrated culture as an institution elevated above the people," Howells asserted the hegemony of the democratic "high average," sustained by a literarily informed and engaged reading public.[74] But he also admitted a doubt whether the workings of the literary marketplace might not drag down that standard to the egalitarian banality of the lowest common denominator. When the gods and half-gods and even heroes go, perhaps the literary hucksters arrive, at a level below even that of Winston Churchill and his best-selling ilk.

It was in this respect, perhaps, that Howells later believed his speech—"my farrago of *spropositi*" (absurdities), as he renounced it to James—had been "all, all wrong and unfit." Apparently, however, no one knew it, "not even I till that ghastly waking hour of the night when hell opens to us" (*SL*, 6:16). Having already heard alarming accounts of the event, James commiserated with his old friend about "the terrible banquet (for I think it must indeed have been terrible,) . . . an ordeal for you of the 1st water (or I suppose *wine;*) through which, not less clearly, you passed unscathed as to your grace & humour & taste."[75]

As Howells's hellish phantasm suggested, he had not emerged unscathed; the full horror of the ordeal came later, after the vinous fumes and the rhetorical gas had cleared away, in that imaginative time and space F. Scott Fitzgerald would later describe as the "real dark night of the soul" where it is "always three o'clock in the morning, day after day."[76] Here the primal dread, as Howells explained to James, was part and parcel of "the divine madness of an affair [the Birthday dinner] in which I still struggle to identify my accustomed self" (*SL*, 6:16).[77]

Lewis P. Simpson has interpreted Howells's "crisis of identity" over the 1912 banquet as a manifestation of his self-division between two "opposing images deeply entangled in his consciousness: a vision of an ideal and sacred American literary order and a counter, nightmarish vision of the actual, corrupt disorder of the American literary life."[78] In his own speech Howells had summoned the sacerdotal cult, those who once had laid apostolic hands upon him, as if to bear witness to his own Deanly apotheosis. But for all of its high-cultural trappings, this dinner had been no sacramental ritual. Howells found himself (if he really *was* himself) at a command performance by The Dean of American Letters—"something," as he had told his brother, "I could not refuse"[79]—for the commercial benefit of the House of Harper.

To Howells himself the greatest of his birthday tributes arrived two months later, in the form of some remarks attributed to Leo Tolstoy by a correspondent of Henry Demarest Lloyd (a legal crusader for progressive causes):

> Howells he seemed to like on account of what he called his "fine spirit"—as well as his manner of writing. As we walked—the count is a good tramper—he suddenly exclaimed, "There are four men in this world that I should like to be the means of bringing together," and my recollection is that three of the four were you [H. D. Lloyd], Mr. [Henry] George and Mr. Howells.

"Think of my having to stand such praise as this from Tolstoy," Howells exulted to his son John. "Pretty good for a little novelist, what, from the greatest that ever lived?"[80] To Tolstoy's small gathering of like minds, which rested secure in the imagination of the world's greatest novelist, no members of the press were invited.

V

A DEAD CULT

Unmaking "The Dean"

ON 2 MARCH 1913, the anniversary of the Harper banquet, Howells gratefully acknowledged the seventy-sixth birthday greetings of his editor, Frederick A. Duneka. "I consider that in all decency I ought not to [have] lagged on after that glorious celebration last year," he joked, "and perhaps I really am dead. In that case it is the voice of posterity hailing me from Franklin Square and giving me a sense of posthumous glory" (*SL*, 6:31).[1] This was, perhaps, an intimation of Henry James's prophecy, in his 1912 tribute, that Howells's "really beautiful time will come."[2] But in 1915, writing to James, Howells now appraised himself as "comparatively a dead cult with my statues cast down and the grass growing over them in the pale moonlight" (*SL*, 6:80).

Neither the vision of posthumous glory nor the vision of pacific neglect contemplated the violence of the assault to come. During the second decade of the new century, says Edwin H. Cady, a myth accreted around The Dean, now turned Academician: "His friends began, disastrously, to sentimentalize that 'dear old saint,' as Brand Whitlock called him."[3] The voice of posterity hailed this mythic figure with contempt. Not content to cast down The Dean's statues and leave the moonlit grass to blanket them, the moderns dragged the dread icons into broad daylight and smashed them to smithereens.

In 1903, Howells got a preview of this bleak future from a revisitation of the past. Charles Eliot Norton lent him some early letters of Henry James, including his unflattering comments about *Their Wedding Journey* upon its serial publication. "Poor Howells is certainly difficult to defend if one takes a stand-point the least bit exalted," James opined to Grace Norton in 1871; "make any serious demands and it's all up with him. He presents, I confess, to my mind, a somewhat melancholy spectacle—in that his charming style and refined intentions are so poorly and meagerly served by our American atmosphere." Howells, James surmised with the sublime egoism of his ruthlessly competitive youth, had already "passed into the stage which I suppose is the eventual fate of all secondary and tertiary talents—worked off his less slender Primitive, found a place and a routine and an income, and now is destined to fade slowly and softly away in self-repetition and reconcilement to the common-place." Still and all, James vouchsafed that Howells will "always be a *writer* —small but genuine" (*SL*, 5:55 n).

With estimable self-possession, Howells thanked Norton for disclosing this and other letters that must have cut him deeply. "I think their criticism very just," he evenly replied; "I have often thought my intellectual raiment was more than my intellectual body, and that I might finally be convicted, not of having nothing *on*, but that worse nakedness of having nothing *in*" (*SL*, 5:54). But then he defended himself. If his use of his gift—his crystalline style—had been, as James put it, "like a poor man with a diamond which he does not know what to do with," then he might agree he *had* mostly "cut rather inferior window glass with it."[4] But he made no apologies "for having wrought in common, crude material so much; that is the right American stuff." His conscious purpose, then and now, was "trying to fashion a piece of literature out of the life next at hand" (*SL*, 5:54).

I

THESE WERE precisely the grounds, however, on which The Dean was first attacked by the younger generation. At no time during his long career did Howells ever escape criticism, and the nature of the criticism remained consistent insofar as it was inflected by romantic assumptions and centered on the perceived deficiencies of realism as a literary method. However, whereas at the height of Howells's success, during the 1880s, his fiction had sometimes been seen as provocative and denounced as excessively analytic or perilously agnostic, the complaint against The Dean, soon after the turn of the century, was the banality, placidity, and "femininity" of his all too common and crude material.

For the California novelist Gertrude Atherton, who may be taken as representative of Howells's critics in the next generation, the idea of the life next at hand was the *wrong* American stuff. Realism, which Atherton renamed "Littleism" in a 1904 essay, had produced an American literature that is "the most timid, the most anaemic, the most lacking in individualities, the most bourgeois, that any country has ever known." Left completely out of account has been "American independence, impatience, energy, contempt of ancient convention": the qualities characteristic not of the Howellsian high average, but rather of a natural aristocracy of virile (that is, "masculine") adventurers whose extraordinary reality demands a full-bloodedly romantic treatment. Littleism is just too middling:

> It is the expression of that *bourgeoisie* which is afraid of doing the wrong thing, not of the indifferent aristocrat; of that element that dares not use slang, shrinks from audacity, rarely utters a bold sentiment and as rarely feels one. It is as correct as Sunday clothes and as innocuous as sterilized milk, but it is not aristocratic. The natural result of its success is, that American writers feel no necessity to see the world.[5]

Atherton's argument seconded Frank Norris' contemporaneous manifesto for moving beyond realism. "The reason why one claims so much for Romance, and quarrels so pointedly with Realism," Norris urged in "A Plea for Romantic Fiction," is that Realism stultifies itself. It notes only the surface of things." Howells's novels, which are as "respectable as a church and proper as a deacon," concern merely "the drama of a broken teacup, the tragedy of a walk down the block, the excitement of an afternoon call, the adventure of an invitation to dinner."[6]

Although Atherton did not take aim directly or exclusively at Howells, his image served as her symbolic bull's-eye. She recalled how a picture of his study, clipped from some magazine, was mounted on cardboard and "enthroned" on her own desk, as if Howells were presiding both as the muse and as The Dean. "At this time he was the controlling force in American letters," Atherton asserts. Although his novels "dealt too much with the small side of daily life to appeal to my temperament and demands," she nonetheless "read them dutifully, with becoming humility." She had "caught the Howells fever and was even a little awed."[7] Not for long. But the Dean's authority continued to cast a chilling shadow over the exuberance of her rebellious spirit.

Much the same reaction was attributed to the suicidal poet-hero of Upton Sinclair's early novel, *The Journal of Arthur Stirling* (1903). Author of a supposedly brilliant (and therefore unpublishable) verse drama titled "The Captive," Stirling at one point copies into his journal the "simply blasphemous" opinion, attributed to Howells, that "the whole belief in genius seems to me rather a mischievous superstition, and if not mischievous, always, still always, a superstition." Stirling retorts: "Genius is next to the last and most sacred word we know, next to God."[8] One cause of the poet's hopelessness is the indifference of a prominent writer to whom he has turned for aid and comfort against those philistine publishers who have rejected "The Captive." Although this literary authority is never identified by name, his fictive role inevitably recalls The Dean's in the real publishing world. In the novel, however, the older writer's reputation for integrity and idealism proves to be unfounded; he offers only cynical advice, attuned to the exigencies of the literary marketplace.

Like Sinclair, Jack London also questioned the legitimacy of Howells's authority, casting him as the fatuous Vanderwater in *Martin Eden* (1909), another novel about the depredations of the publishing world. "You worship at the shrine of the established," Martin scoffs at the sanctimoniously respectable Ruth Morse. "Every school teacher in the land looks up to Vanderwater as the Dean of American criticism. Yet I read his stuff, and it seems to me the perfection of the felicitous expression of the inane. Why, he is no more than a ponderous bromide, thanks to Gelett Burgess."[9] Like Arthur Stirling, Martin Eden eventually kills himself in despair over the corruption of genius by the bloodsucking and soul-destroying business of authorship.

Atherton, like London, made it plain that her rejection of "Littleism" was ultimately a form of resistance to the monopoly of the literary establishment, which mandated tribute to its "old superstitions" as the price for breaking into print. "The big magazines and their houses will publish nothing that does not conform to the standard which has weathered other upheavals," she alleged, and the newspapers ape the literary opinions of the big magazines. Those authors who have "defied the powers and won an honorable position independent of any temporary demand" are, in fact, "so few in number that they rather terrify than encourage the youthful aspirant: their fight has been too long and arduous, and that other way lies sure, if no very brilliant, success."[10]

Implicit in Atherton's critique was the perception of Howells as a tool of an oppressively inbred cultural regime. This idea found explicit (but also humorous) expression in *The Literary Guillotine* (1903), a satire with the amusing premise of imagining various popular writers hauled before the bar of justice for their literary crimes and sentenced accordingly, or else embroiled in arcane literary litigations. Thus, for instance, the presiding judges of this kangaroo court (Mark Twain, Oliver Herford, and the anonymous narrator) hear the "infringement of patent" suit brought by Henry James against Mary Baker Eddy, ruling that "the original *sententia obscura,* containing, as its name implies, a palpable though obfuscated idea, is not infringed by a method of compilation by which the idea, if any, is placed absolutely beyond the reach of discovery."[11]

Howells appears only in the last chapter, which is a rollicking debate among several authors about the "identity of literature and business" (p. 238). Here a buffoonish Howells is portrayed—as if in confirmation of the poetess Mary Arnold Child's horrendous pun, "Thy fame is reckoned with the harpers, still" (see note 6)—as little more than a shill for Franklin Square. Howells, it seems, devotes his column to puffing and peddling his publisher's wares. When asked by Mark Twain to suggest some way to save literature, Howells replies:

> "Simply this—let [Richard Harding] Davis go hang, he doesn't publish with Harper's any longer. Release [John Kendrick] Bangs from the asylum [to which he has been consigned by the court], and substitute [Brander] Matthews. The Professor's books don't sell, anyhow."
>
> "I see, Mr. Howells. Certainly no one can accuse you of not taking a practical view of literature."
>
> "No one, sir. That's what my boss always says to me. 'Mr. Howells,' he said only the other day, 'the Easy Chair is the best advertising medium Harper's possesses. The way you manage to ring in our books while apparently writing on matters literary, is a subject for constant wonder.' " (Pp. 249–50)

The impact of *The Literary Guillotine* obviously depended on exaggeration. But was Howells *really* guilty of literary logrolling in the "Easy Chair"? A check of his first year's columns (December 1900 to December 1901) shows that he reviewed thirteen books, eight in a single month (October), all but two of which were novels. No publishers were identified in the magazine, but six of the thirteen books (five of the eleven novels) were, in fact, Harper and Brothers titles. No other publisher was represented more than once, except McClure, Phillips (twice). There was also a preponderance of Howellsian friends and protégés among the authors reviewed: Henry James, Nathaniel Shaler, Edith Wyatt, Edith Wharton, Henry Blake Fuller, Frank Norris, and Vaughn Kester (who was a distant relation as well!).[12] It would appear, then, that *The Literary Guillotine* had a prima facie case; although Howells was sentenced to no punishment worse than ridicule, the audacity of the indictment suggests some slippage in his unassailability.

The Dean seemed even more vulnerable in 1907, when Atherton renewed her attack on his tameness and insipidity, and William Lyon Phelps, a popular Yale professor, leaped to defend him from such a "violent revolt against his leadership." Atherton had charged (in Phelps's paraphrase) "that Mr. Howells has been and is a writer for boarding-school misses; that he has never penetrated deeply into life; and that not only has his own timidity prevented him from courageously revealing the hearts of men and women, but that his position of power and influence has cast a blight on American fiction." On the contrary, Phelps insisted, we should be grateful for Howells's "Reticent Realism" as "a silent but emphatic protest against 'mentioning the unmentionable.'" It has shielded Americans from the corruption of decadent Continental fiction: "do we really wish to see young men and women, boys and girls, reading stories that deal mainly with sex?" Whereas "many a struggling young writer has cause to bless him for powerful assistance," Atherton impudently and imprudently abets literary malcontents, "who lack her wisdom and experience, and whose chief dislike of Mr. Howells, when finally analysed, seems to be directed against his intense ethical earnestness."[13]

What's notable here is the high seriousness with which Phelps, as paladin of American gentility, took these criticisms of Howells and their hint of a wider "revolt" against precious American pieties incarnate in The Dean. Compared to Howells, a literary colossus, Atherton might well have been regarded as a mosquito, against whose annoying buzz and bite he should scarcely have *needed* protection (especially by a flyswatting third party). But rebellion was definitely in the air, as Phelps alertly sensed. If Howells had been inclined to defend himself, he was now prevented by his own exalted status, with which only regal silence seemed commensurate. Thus as The Dean became more and more monumentalized, a paralyzing petrification set in, leaving Howells immured in the prisonhouse of his own celebrity, impotent to conserve his rapidly diminishing power.

II

ANOTHER TELLING instance of Howells's weakened authority, also in the context of loyal service to his publishers, was the debacle of *The Whole Family,* a collectively authored serial novel, originally meant to exemplify the principles of Howellsian realism by depicting an archetypal American family "in middling circumstances, of average culture and experiences" (*SL,* 5:180). In the spring of 1906, Howells suggested the project to Elizabeth Jordan, editor of *Harper's Bazar,* in part as "a showplace for Harper's family of authors."[14] Each author would contribute one chapter, from the first-person point of view of one member of an extended family comprising a father and mother, the mother's mother, the father's unmarried sister, a married son and daughter and their respective spouses, an adolescent girl, a schoolboy, and a marriageable young lady, whose pending engagement might serve as the "moment of vital agitation" (*SL,* 5:179–80) that would propel the plot—any loose ends to be tied up in a final chapter by a family friend.[15]

Rounding up contributors—the work of coordination fell to Jordan—proved to be more difficult than expected. The final team, including only about half of those originally sought, consisted of Howells and Jordan themselves, three established New England authors (Mary E. Wilkins Freeman, Elizabeth Stuart Phelps, and Alice Brown), four promising but relatively unknown women writers (Mary Heaton Vorse, Mary Stewart Cutting, Edith Wyatt, and Mary R. Shipman Andrews), the popular humorist John Kendrick Bangs, the equally popular moralist Henry van Dyke, and (somewhat incongruously) Henry James.

It was Jordan's idea to invite James to participate; Howells had suggested that neither he nor Edith Wharton would likely be interested. It may have been the inclusion of James, after all, that was decisive for keeping Howells himself involved.[16] Conscious of his Deanly dignity, he had warned Jordan: "If you find the scheme does not commend itself to the more judicious and able among the writers to whom you propose it, you had better drop it. I should not like to appear in co-operation with young or unimportant writers" (*SL,* 5:181 n).

Howells conceived a serious, and even didactic, purpose for *The Whole Family.* Inspired, perhaps, by the painfully broken engagement of his daughter Mildred, he wanted to see the novel explore the idea that "an engagement or a marriage is much more a family affair, and much less a personal affair than Americans usually suppose." He wished, moreover, to advocate coeducation as a means of narrowing the perceived differences between the sexes—differences "exaggerated by the separate training"—and of promoting better knowledge of "the workings of the male and female mind" (*SL,* 5:180 n).

Despite Howells's high-minded intentions, *The Whole Family* was pitched to the public as a literary novelty and sacrificed to trade considerations. With its heavy concentration of female talent, the novel matched the readership of *Harper's Bazar.*

As the serial chapters appeared anonymously (but with an accompanying list of contributors), the "intelligent reader" was teasingly flattered to suppose that she would "experience no difficulty in determining which author wrote each chapter—perhaps" (*WF,* xxxv). This guessing game, along with leaks about infighting among the contributors did, in fact, produce the desired gossip and publicity in the New York literary press. The frankly commercial thrust of the project was typical of popular magazines in the period, part of the new editorial order in which contents were often determined in advance by trend-conscious editors and then parceled to writers more or less as piecework.

In general, the writers were well paid—as were those contributors to *The Whole Family* who were aware enough of their market value to demand their due. Even the neophyte Mary Stewart Cutting insisted on $350, only $50 less than the $400 in which James professed to take "perfect satisfaction," but far below the $750 top fee that Phelps commanded. Next was van Dyke at $600; Brown asked for $500. Freeman received a mere $250, "her usual sum for a short story"; and Howells earned nothing, as his chapter was covered by his Harper house salary (*WF,* xviii). The pay scale, in other words, expressed a differential not of literary accomplishment or reputation so much as of self-assessed worth in the marketplace.

As the range of payment suggests, the authorial parties to *The Whole Family* made their separate deals and then acted accordingly in writing their respective chapters, giving small latitude either to each other's imaginative initiatives or to Howells's overarching motive. One big problem was the chapter on the Mother submitted by Edith Wyatt, Howells's midwestern protégé, who would never have been asked to join *The Whole Family* without his advocacy. By adopting an epistolary format rather than a first-person point of view, Wyatt's chapter threatened the book's narrative integrity.

Duneka was apoplectic. The chapter, he seethed to Jordan, was "simply awful—confused, dull, stupid, vapid, meaningless, halting, lame, holding up the action and movement of the story which has run along so splendidly thus far." Such "cruelly incompetent drivel" was "simply awful"; the author should be paid off and then unceremoniously dumped from the project. But when Wyatt resisted her expulsion, Jordan allowed her to rewrite the offending chapter. The result in Howells's eyes was "charming—delicately true to nature and abounding in fine bits of observation." But Howells always had a blind spot for Wyatt, in whose work he could never seem to interest anyone else. James was much closer to the truth in abhorring her reduction of the Mother to "a positive small convulsion of debility—without irony, without fancy, without anything!"[17] Although the rankest criticism of Wyatt was channeled to Jordan, Howells likely got wind of it too. He must have been embarrassed by the perceived ineptitude of a young writer he had backed so unreservedly. Nevertheless, the Wyatt imbroglio was by no means the severest blow to The Dean's dignity.

Not surprisingly, given its audience and its means of production, *The Whole*

Family became a predictable formula fiction. As van Dyke's Friend of the Family purrs in the concluding chapter, "Everything has turned out just as it should, like a romance in an old-fashioned ladies' magazine" (*WF,* 303). What's interesting about the novel is how it occasionally strains against its own conformity to the conventions of popular romance. To be sure, the courtship of Peggy Talbert dominates the plot, which in turn dominates most of the characters in a way that Howells had not desired and later deplored. But some of the writers of *The Whole Family* resisted the literary codes, either by subverting them through ingenious twists of plot or turns of character, or by foregrounding them in ways that reflexively call attention to their own fictionality.[18]

The subversion came early. Writing a first chapter sketchy enough to leave room for later developments, Howells expected the others to follow suit. His plans were deranged, however, in the second chapter, written by Freeman. She had taken offense at Howells's antiquated conception of the Aunt, in a narrative comment that "Miss Talbert was not without the [romantic] disappointment which endears maiden ladies to the imagination" (*WF,* 19). Deducing that the Aunt was a mere thirty-four, Freeman, who at the age of fifty had recently married a younger man, discarded the spinster stereotype and created, as Jordan said, "an up-and-coming character, attractive, and modern in dress and ideas."[19] Freeman cast Miss Elizabeth Talbert as a sexually vital woman who believes that "an old-maid aunt is as much of an anomaly as a spinning-wheel" (*WF,* 33) and who fantasies that she "might yet be captured as the Sabine women were" (*WF,* 43). A connoisseur of adventures too erotic and travels too exotic by local community standards, Lily (as she is known outside her brother's village) has most recently been romantically entangled with the Young Man who is engaged to her niece Peggy!

"Heavens! what a catastrophe! Who would have thought that the maiden aunt would go mad in the second chapter?" van Dyke exclaimed to Jordan. "For my part I think it distinctly crewel work to put a respectable spinster into such a hattitude before the world," he added punningly. "What *will* Mr. Howells say?" Mr. Howells, in a letter that Jordan later said had "almost scorched the paper it was written on," said: "Don't, *don't* let her ruin our beautiful story!" But Jordan strongly identified herself with Freeman's conception of Aunt Lily, remarking: "I myself was in my thirties and convinced that I was going strong." It was impossible, in any event, to reject "one of Harper's most valued and successful authors." In concurrence with Duneka, Colonel Harvey, and Henry Mills Alden, she also saw a (selling) point to Freeman's chapter: it provided the "push" the novel needed "for cumulative interest."[20] So The Dean was politely overruled by the management at Franklin Square. Not only was the Freeman chapter allowed to stand; the controversial Aunt became the new focal point of *The Whole Family.*

Jordan strongly hints that Harper's progressive editorial team regarded Howells as a fuddy-duddy (a word of recent coinage): someone to be treated with exaggerated deference that belies knowing indifference to his unstylish opinions. This was the drift of Jordan's account of how the contributors had reacted to Howells's opening chapter, the proofs of which she had distributed: "They all read his introduction, however, with the interest and respect due to the work of the Dean of American Literature." In the end, however, Jordan and the others ignored his wishes in the name of up-to-dateness. Howells "took the decision like the scholar and gentleman he was," she recalled; "but he let me see that he thought the novel was wrecked and that he himself lay buried among the ruins."[21]

III

THE WHOLE FAMILY affair and the attacks by Atherton and other members of the younger (but not the youngest) generation suggest that The Dean's premature burial amid the ruins of a dead cult was already well advanced during the Age of Howells. As Cady suggests, the process accelerated once The Dean devolved into the Academician. "It became a fashion to blast away critically at Howells without having bothered to read him"; and since his creative years were all but over, "that settled habit of ignorance in the young men made it impossible for the Academician to direct their view back toward his real achievement and meaning."[22]

It is ironic that some of the worst damage was inflicted by someone who *had* read him: someone, indeed, who adulated Howells as "the greatest living artist in the field of fiction who uses the English language," even "as great a literary artist as Balzac, greater from that point of view than Thackeray or George Eliot or Tolstoy, or Kipling." These and many other outlandish claims appeared in Alexander Harvey's *William Dean Howells* (1917), the first book-length study ever published of Howells's career.[23] Often the appearance of such a book marks a signal moment in the history of a literary reputation: when a writer begins to move, if at all, beyond his or her own time, when the case for a writer's enduring claim on posterity finds its earliest, sometimes its best, articulation. As Howells himself wrote to one of Harvey's colleagues upon receipt of the book, which its author had shied from sending himself, "a man does not have a whole volume written about him, whether of praise or blame, or both, as this is, without great inward stir" (*SL*, 6:119).

Unfortunately, the inward stir for Howells must have been nauseating as the volume's consummate asininity revealed itself page by page, culminating in a baroque index designed to "throw off the shackles" of Doctor Dry-as-dust and provide a model for indexes "we shall want to read for their pith, their point, their provocativeness" (p. 233). As noted by a reviewer for the *Dial*, "The author's text is not so much a book as a tirade, not so much a tirade as a miscellany, and not so much a miscellany as the preface to an index. . . . We ask for bread and are given—by no means a stone, but, let us say, a cocktail."[24] Long on provocation but very short on pith and point, *William Dean Howells* lurched free-associatively from one thought to another, occasionally coming briefly to reeling rest in the general vicinity of its ostensible topic, otherwise tossing off dogmatic opinions on everything else and ventilating pet peeves. And toward Howells himself Harvey expressed contradictory attitudes, praising the perfection of his character-drawing while, like Atherton, blaming him for "the 'sissy' school" of realism that had "rendered contemporary American literature a thin syrup, perfumed to a feminized taste" (p. 206). Like *The Literary Guillotine,* the book also censured The Dean's association with Franklin Square: "what can have induced Howells to enter the pay of the Harpers? Was it money? I suppose so. Well, that house of Harper put the blight of its own literary superstitions—all British—upon Howells and to that extent it ruined the author" (p. 248).[25]

The maddeningly improvisatory and digressive nature of what one reviewer called "this farrago of impertinences and irrelevancies" is suggested by its running heads, printed in huge type at the top of each odd (in both senses!) page. Here, for example, are the running heads for a chapter titled "The Purity of the Women of Howells," which begins by mentioning Howells and then largely ignores him thereafter: "Living Life," "Wordsworth," "Woman," "The Lady," "Passion," "Heroines." As Francis Hackett said of Harvey, "it is abundantly clear from the start that Mr Howells is his point of departure rather than his goal." Or, as the *New York Times* put it, "Occasionally you meet with an experience or a thing for which some particular word is the one fit and perfect definition. So with this book. For it the word egregious seems to have been exquisitely invented."

William Dean Howells mortified its involuntary subject, who reported that reading it was "like looking at myself a long time in a mirror where I saw some one of my name and work powerfully reflected, and being possessed with the doubt whether it was really I" (*SL,* 6:119). To his old friend Thomas Sergeant Perry, Howells confessed:

> After a first look into it I thought I could not bear to read it, yet did so finally, in spite of my small stomach for things about me. First he skies me, inordinately, and then drivels over me with talk about "sissyism." All of us, it seems, who are not drunken blackguards are sissies, and I the worst for having kept our authorship sober, as editor and critic. Of course you have seen what the book is, and there is no use telling you. I cannot help being glad he values some characters of mine; but I am no such prodigy as two thirds of his book makes me out; I warn you of that. Still, my curiosity haunts about him. Perhaps he will answer my letter to his pub[lisher]. (*SL,* 6:120)

Harvey, a journalist who had held editorial posts at the *Literary Digest,* the *New York Herald,* and other papers, settled down as associate editor of *Current Opinion* in 1905. He brought to the study of Howells an impressively wide range of literary interests. Himself the author of one book of stories (*The Toe and Other Tales* [1913]), Harvey had translated classical texts by Sophocles, Euripides, Aristophanes,

Terence, Plautus, and Seneca, as well as Nietzsche's *Human, All Too Human* (1908). In 1906, he had also published a brief life of Robert Louis Stevenson for a reprint of *A Child's Garden of Verses* and an introduction to *Treasure Island.* Harvey's next project after *William Dean Howells* was *Shelley's Elopement: A Study of the Most Romantic Episode in Literary History* (1918); he would later contribute several small volumes to the Haldeman-Julius Company's populist series of Pocket Books and Little Blue Books: *Essays on Sophocles, Essays on Aeschylus,* and *Essays on Euripides* in 1923; *Essays on Jesus* and *Essays on the Friends of Jesus* in 1924.

Thus although Harvey's book on Howells was certainly ludicrous, its author was no fool; and when Howells finally met him face to face late in 1917, he was shocked to discover that Harvey (1868–1949) was "not the callow ass's colt we figured him, but a staid old horse of fifty with a son in the army" (*SL,* 6:123 n). What saddle burr, then, had sent this nag galloping round the bend? At some point during the composition of his study, Harvey, like many other American intellectuals at the time, was convulsed by a Freudian conversion experience. The scales dropped from his eyes, and he now could see what he had no doubt been repressing: "the art of Howells is barren" (p. 217):

> To tell the truth, it is impossible to read the literature of the psychoanalytic school of Freudian psychology without marveling at the completeness with which the whole fabric of the Howells criticism collapses and disintegrates. It is all surface and no depth.
>
> Howells, then, has done an enormous amount of damage to American literature. He was enabled to do all the mischief through the medium of his own amazing genius in technique, his own perfect humor, his mastery of dialogue, his ability to reflect the lives of the native Americans of Anglo-Saxon origin. These people have never explored life subjectively. The American subconsciousness is to all intents and purposes a sealed book. The poverty of the American Anglo-Saxon mind consists in this very superficiality, this strict adherence to the surface of life. (pp. 202–3)

Through Freudian lenses, the ideals of Howellsian realism—using "common, crude material," the right American stuff, "to fashion a piece of literature out of the life next at hand" (*SL,* 5:54)—became not merely superficial and psychologically naive, but also profoundly neurotic. Unlike the virile, drunken Poe, who delves into the "subconsciousness" and "insinuates the sorcery of sex with refinement, subtly" (pp. 220–21), the effeminized Howells, as the ringleader of the "sissy" school of American fiction, is barren and also, as it were, frigid—sexually repressed and repressive.

Inchoate here was the modern critique of Howells that would soon become a commonplace. Harvey, like his near contemporary Sherwood Anderson, acted as an advance scout for the mustering Freudian army that would soon put Howells and his fellow sissies to rout.[26] As I have already suggested (in chapter 3), the gendering of Howells as "effeminate" (as in Norris' caricature of Howellsian realism as "the drama of a broken teacup") became a favorite tactic for defaming him. Among many examples is John Macy's contention that if life is a tempest in a teapot, then the "feminine, delicate, slightly romantic" Howells was "one of its finest and most faithful recorders. But he puts the emphasis on the teapot and not on the tempest, which is hardly consonant with his often restated, almost militant declaration that literature is life."[27]

It is, of course, another commonplace to note the often violent reaction during the early years of the twentieth century against the supposed "feminization" of American culture. Even someone as genteel as Alden, the real editor of *Harper's Monthly*, with his finger on the pulse of its predominantly female readership, could sympathize with those perturbed by the dominance of women in the literary arena: "But there is no sterility like that of a feminized culture, unruffled by the masculine spirit, vexed to its depths only by its own feverish unrest. There is in it no sense of the morning, of the springtime, no token of renascence."[28]

By contrast, Harvey's rant about "the 'sissy' school" and Howells's maidenly repression was crude, but his formulations sent a shock of recognition through still younger writers groping for terms to express their hatred of The Dean and the Victorian ethos he seemed so inexorably to enforce upon them. Howells, for his part, blithely confirmed the moderns' darkest imaginings about his sex life, past or present. Before meeting with Harvey in December 1917, Howells sent him a self-defensive letter in which he readily labeled himself "an old fogey (as we used to say)" and then denounced the whole idea of de-repression, as it was widely (mis)understood by Freud's American disciples:

> I respect that passion [love] in young people if it inspires them to marriage, but otherwise it can only at best have my pity. It is then the source of more unhappiness than anything else in the world, and I wish people to be happy, just as I wish them to be good. . . .
>
> I am sure I am right in desiring always to be decent. I know we are naked under our clothes but I know we have always our clothes on unless we are savages. (*SL*, 6:122)

Here was the prissy old maid (the antithesis to Freeman's sexy Aunt Lily!) that H. L. Mencken had pilloried, in his January 1917 review of *The Leatherwood God* (1916), as "Agnes Repplier in pantaloons": a vastly overrated writer, wrapped in "a web of superstitious reverence," whose unread books are fawned over by "the lady critics of the newspapers," who would "no more question them than they would question Lincoln's Gettysburg speech, or Paul Elmer More, or their own virginity." This was "The Dean," as Mencken smartly renamed him, insolently clipping the title of this "member of the literary peerage, and of the rank of earl at least." The Dean was "an urbane and highly respectable old gentleman, a sitter on committees, an intimate of professors and the prophets of movements, a worthy vouched for by both the *Atlantic Monthly* and Alexander Harvey, a placid conformist."

Although, like Harvey, Mencken was prepared to concede that Howells was an admirable stylist who had rescued American English from British pomposity, he also judged the fiction to be "elegant and shallow," devoid of any sniff of the underlying "universal mystery": "The profound dread and agony of life, the surge of passion and aspiration, the grand crash and glitter of things, the tragedy that runs eternally under the surface." Mencken nowhere mentions psychoanalysis in his diatribe, but Howells is implicitly faulted for lacking the saving insight of the Freudian dispensation, which might have redeemed his character-drawing from being so "superficial, amateurish, often nonsensical." His portrait of Dylks, the Leatherwood God, for instance, is "not a 'study' at all, whether psychological or otherwise, but simply an anecdote, and without either point or interest." Unlike Norris or Dreiser, Howells is incapable of evoking the "race-spirit" or "the essential conflict of forces among us, of the peculiar drift and color of American life."[29]

A more complete damnation cannot be easily imagined. Mencken shoved The Dean off his pedestal and brought down his reputation in a single stroke. Mencken's caricature of Howells was all the more devastating for being so recklessly unfair and so hilariously memorable! Furthermore, Mencken's brash act of lèse-majesté emboldened the restive youngest generation of barely postadolescent moderns, who had previously left the literary combat to their elders, such as Atherton or Harvey.

IV

THROUGHOUT THE teens and twenties, the leading spokesman for the new generation of American writers and the critic with the greatest influence on his contemporaries was undoubtedly Van Wyck Brooks. "Perhaps more effectively than any other prophet of the Modern," Cady says, "Brooks laid waste Howells's reputation." The devastation was so total because Brooks and so many other Howells antagonists "came out of the Bohemian, but more especially the Harvard-esthetic school" and avowed its belief "that no artistic America existed."[30] This tenet lay at the heart of Brooks's denunciations of The Dean.

At first, however, Brooks, like Atherton, had stood in awe of Howells. In 1907, soon after finishing Harvard (in three years) and moving to New York, the ambitious young man, aged twenty-one, laid siege to The Dean at his hotel. "I wished to put to him the preposterous question, how should one set about being a writer," Brooks later recalled, in the guise of Oliver Allston. Was it expedient to work for a newspaper? (this was the conventional wisdom at Harvard) assuming, of course, that one would be writing editorials. Howells softly replied that "this was like joining the army with the expectation of being a general at the outset."[31]

Brooks could have been taking his cues from the "Editor's Easy Chair" of November 1904, where Howells, through his persona Eugenio, had noted how as he "grew older, and became, rightfully or wrongfully, more and more widely known for his writings, he found himself increasingly the subject of appeals from young writers who wished in their turn to become, rightfully or wrongfully, more and more widely known." Some of these petitioners, in fact, were not *yet* writers; "they had only the ambition to be writers." But they all wished, in any case, "to know one thing: namely, how he did it." What, after all, was his secret, "his recipe for making the kind of literature which had made him famous"? And they all wanted to start at the top. "The perception of this fact made Eugenio very sad, and he asked himself if the willingness to arrive only after you had got there had gone out of the world and left nothing but the ambition to be at this point or that without the trouble of having reached it."[32]

Brooks soon proved he was not averse to building a career through hard work, but in 1907 he did not know quite what to make of Howells. He had offered no help about journalism, Brooks reported to his fiancée, but he was "ever so nice and genial, and made up in good feeling for what he lacked in advice. But such a funny little round-shouldered *bunch* of a man! —He almost rolled about the floor rather than walked, and his kind face was like crepe for wrinkles!" This description was not meant unkindly, Brooks continued; "for I would give a great deal for the proper words to tell how cordial and good-humoured and sympathetic he was."[33] But there was unmistakable aggression underlying Brooks's supposed admiration for Howells: an ambivalence that gradually deepened into open hostility. Although many years later Brooks would find himself "drawn almost as deeply to him as to William James," Howells became a nemesis for the young Brooks: a relict of "an Anglo-American past that seemed now almost as remote as the past of Persia," the symbol of everything that he thought was wrong with American life.[34]

Two years later, having done his Grub Street apprenticeship and earned a job as editorial assistant at *The World's Work,* a far more cagey and polished Brooks returned to Howells for an interview—though the reporter did most of the talking. Brooks was investigating a paradox: that while "Mr. William Dean Howells has never surprised anybody, thrilled anybody, shocked anybody," and while his career and his works alike "seem devoid of inspired moments," still the "very people who would be first to call his work mediocre are those who instinctively recognize in him a unique distinction." This distinction consisted in his preference for the light of common day—"It is only rare minds who are impressed by common things"—and as ordinary readers are seldom interested in "the true, immediate, actual things that make up life," Howells's audience was necessarily small.[35]

Brooks seemed to be testing Howells, probing to discover if he were merely a writing machine and thus incapable of passionate immensities and intensities.

The first (trick) question set the tone: "Do you ever find that you have lost yourself in your work, that your characters get the better of you, that your own feelings become entangled?" "Never," Howells replied, walking into the trap. "The essence of achievement is to keep outside, to be entirely dispassionate, as a sculptor must be, moulding his clay" (p. 88). Howells insisted that even such writers as Dickens, who appear to wear their hearts on their sleeves, are merely good actors; they are always really in control. Did Howells ever get distracted? Could he suffer interruptions? He had been writing for fifty years, he said, and nothing interfered with his work habits.

Brooks insinuated a doubt, seemingly based on Howells's own responses, about the true caliber of his literary intelligence:

> It is a mind which has held itself in mastery over all its creations, a little too fastidious to be eccentric. Is there not in this, perhaps, the explanation of a certain lack of force, a lack of that which compels readers and is characteristic of the supreme novelists as well as of those who have a great popularity for the moment? True as his novels are, a unique mirror of all the common things of life, one rebels against them, as one rebels against the common things themselves. One feels that in standing away from his characters to mass them properly, he has focused them all in a group very far away, so that all appear the same size, and all under middle height. (P. 89)

The subtle undercutting of Howells, which pervades the interview, is especially effective toward the end, as Brooks points to evidence of The Dean's authorial diligence: the little bookcase beside the plain writing table, which holds row upon row of Howells's books, in every size and every sort of binding; so many books that they have all but crowded out any but the author's own. It was wonderful to behold them, Brooks exclaims: "In a way it was like standing in the room with a classic; for the nature of Mr. Howells'ss reputation, in whatever degree it has strength and power, is that of a classic—moderate, steady, and perennial" (p. 90). Here is a fine example of damning with faint praise; note the suavely understated reservation about Howells's reputation: "in whatever degree it has strength and power." Here also is the monumentalized Dean as mummy, entombed like some ancient pharaoh along with what might be needed en route to the underworld: plenty of "classic" books to read.

Although Brooks did not hesitate to generalize authoritatively about Howells's novels (as in the condescending aside, "there are not nearly as many young girls who giggle in real life as in Mr. Howells'ss books" [p. 89]), he himself had not at the time actually read more than one of them![36] Brooks was faking it, in a slightly different way from Dreiser a decade earlier. Whereas Dreiser had lifted his 1898 "interview" from Howells's own writings, Brooks, ignorant of that work, was plagiarizing the disdainful opinions about Howells current among "advanced" intellectuals.

These borrowed ideas, honed to an ever sharper edge by an ever keener critical mind, were recycled through Brooks's major works of the late teens, which "brought a whole literary generation into an awareness of itself" by drawing "the profile of their common enemy: puritanic America with its pioneer-commercial mentality, people with stuffy highbrows and insufferable lowbrows." This was, as James R. Vitelli remarks, "something of a fabulous caricature, perhaps, but they recognized the fable as theirs, containing a poetic truth about America as they had experienced it."[37]

In *Letters and Leadership* (1918), Howells was briefly mentioned as author of "the *comedie humaine* of our post-bellum society," a writer who far less than any of his contemporaries "falsified his vision of reality in the interests of popular entertainment." But that vision was naively limited to " 'the more smiling aspects of life' "; Howells believed that "in being true to our 'well-to-do actualities' the American novelist does all that can be expected of him." This, surely, was not enough. "Could one ask for a more essential declaration of artistic bankruptcy than that?" Brooks asked rhetorically.[38]

When Brooks returned to Howells in *The Ordeal of Mark Twain* (1920), his most influential book, The Dean, along with Olivia Clemens, was blamed for taming the unbridled imagination of a great writer and sapping his natural virility. The image Brooks created of Howells as Mark Twain's genteel censor has never been dispelled. Nor has Howells recovered from Brooks's demeaning portrait of him as the exponent of desiccated New England Puritanism. Even more than Mencken's "The Dean," *The Ordeal of Mark Twain* was the wellspring of anti-Howellsian sentiment throughout the 1920s. The crucial passage must be quoted at length in order to capture its cumulative force:

> New England had retained its cultural hegemony by default, and the New England spinster, with her restricted experience, her complicated repressions, and all her glacial taboos of good form, had become the pacemaker in the arts.
>
> One cannot but see in Mr. Howells the predestined figurehead of this new régime. It was the sign of the decay of artistic vitality in New England that the old literary Brahmins were obliged to summon a Westerner to carry on their apostolic succession . . . and certainly Mr. Howells, already intimidated by the prestige of Boston, was a singularly appropriate heir.

Then, once again, Brooks smears Howells—hoist with his own canard—with his allegedly "prime dogma" that "the more smiling aspects of life are the more American."

> [T]he dogma, as we see, was merely a rationalization of his own unconscious desire neither to see in America nor to say about America anything that Americans in general did not wish to have seen or said. His confessed aim was to reveal the charm of

> the commonplace, an essentially passive and feminine conception of his art; and while his superficial realism gave him the sanction of modernity, it dispensed him at the same time from any of those drastic imaginative reconstructions of life and society that are of the essence of all masculine fiction. In short, he had attained a thoroughly denatured point of view and one nicely adapted to an age that would not tolerate any assault upon the established fact: meanwhile, the eminence of his position and his truly beautiful and distinguished talent made him what Mark Twain called "the critical Court of Last Resort in this country, from whose decision there is no appeal." The spokesman, the mild and submissive dictator of an age in which women wrote half the books and formed the greater part of the reading public, he diffused far and wide the notion of the artist's rôle through which he had found his own salvation, a notion, that is to say, which accepted implicitly the religious, moral and social taboos of the time.[39]

Brooks took Harvey's odd crotchets and Mencken's broad satire and reworked them into a well-wrought argument about the inhospitable conditions for art in American culture and, by virtue of his eminent position, The Dean's complicity. All the key notes are struck in *The Ordeal of Mark Twain:* the cultural hegemony of New England and its shriveling Puritanism; the sterilizing feminization of American taste; the failure of "denatured" realism either to penetrate the fastness of the Freudian unconscious or to transcend bourgeois prohibitions. What made the argument so convincing was its psychological sophistication. Howells's supposed blindness to all but the smiling aspects of life, a blindness generalized to bourgeois American culture as a whole, is attributed to an "unconscious desire" not to disturb the psychic balance maintained through repression.[40] In effect, Howells is cast as no less a victim than Mark Twain of the deadly cultural values he supposedly espoused.

V

AS BROOKS'S ideas became widely disseminated during the 1920s, the nuances of his argument were often lost in its adaptation to other critics' polemical purposes. After Brooks, that is, it was open season on The Dean; and in the rough and tumble of Howells-bashing, neatness didn't count and intellectual precision didn't matter.

Even foreign critics joined the fray, and one of them offers a good example of the anti-Howellsian line as it became reduced to a checklist of slogans. In his lectures at the Sorbonne in 1926, Régis Michaud, another zealous convert to psychoanalysis, sneeringly and complacently rehearsed the now familiar litany of Howells's pernicious shortcomings. His psychology was naive and "superficial." His realism was dull and "limited." His American optimism was puerile. His libido was repressed. His mind was warped by "Puritanism." One extended passage may serve as an example for all of what too often passed for Howells criticism in the wake of Mencken and Brooks:

> His ideals were those of the average and banal humanity, of the sentimental middle classes against which American literature is now in revolt. Babbitt himself would have proved too modern, too genial, too "peppy" for Howells. Main Street would be his paradise without Carol Kennicott for a neighbor. Carol was much too progressive and natural for "the Supreme Court of Appeal of American Literature," as Mark Twain liked to call the author of "The Lady of the Aroostook." Howells's ideal people were the Laphams and the Kentons, the dull couples whose lives were wasted in pursuit of commonplace felicity and comfort without any higher ambition than to brood under their wings (if they had any), sons and daughters as dull as they were themselves. Howells's characters do not worry much about subconsciousness. They ran no danger of becoming patients of Doctor Freud. They were much too "normal" for that. A plunge into subconsciousness would have made them unhappy. It would have revealed to them the inanity of their ethics and the lies of their petty lives.[41]

Michaud, who devoted two chapters to Dreiser, also invoked Sinclair Lewis as a hero of those in revolt against the American bourgeoisie.

It was Lewis, of course, acting as the moderns' elder statesman in his Nobel Prize acceptance speech of 1930, who administered the coup de grâce to The Dean. Before Howells, according to Lewis, American literature had no theory of itself and no critical standards. But Howells, regrettably, was a ninny and a genteel prude who gelded Mark Twain, defanged Hamlin Garland, and instilled "The American Fear of Literature." "Mr. Howells was one of the gentlest, sweetest, and most honest of men, but he had the code of a pious old maid whose greatest delight was to have tea at the vicarage." Without tolerance for "the jolly coarseness of life," he imposed a standard of transparently unreal realism in which "farmers and seamen and factory-hands might exist, but the farmer must never be covered with muck, the seaman must never roll out bawdy chanteys, the factory-hand must be thankful to his good employer, and all of them must long for the opportunity to visit Florence and smile gently at the quaintness of the beggars."

Having dispatched Howells, Lewis turned next to "the dean of American letters today," so far as there was one: Hamlin Garland, who before he was "Howellized" had produced the stark prairie stories that anticipated the true midwestern realism of the moderns. Garland, who had lately been grumbling about the decadence of the literary youngsters, was, according to Lewis, Howells's last victim: a potentially great writer who had sold his birthright for the pottage of becoming The Dean's pathetic successor, "the dean." Lewis swelled rhetorically over this cautionary tale: "And it is his tragedy, it is a completely revelatory American tragedy, that in our land of freedom, men like Garland, who first blast the roads to freedom, become themselves the most bound."[42]

But as Lewis finally relieved The Dean of his long empty command, "the dean" received a reminder of what almost everyone was forgetting. Fred Lewis Pattee, one of the pioneers of American literature as an academic discipline, rebuked the amnesia of the moderns, which seemed to be enveloping Garland too:

> It is conventional now to rate Howells as a literary mollycoddle, timid and reactionary, but you and I know how lustily he fought always for the wild native tangs and for that lusty new "he-man" realism which so shocked and alarmed the older mid-century group. It was he who opened the columns of the "Atlantic" for Mark Twain when to the rest of Boston he was but a wild and vulgar Western showman of the Roaring Camp variety. . . .
>
> And how gloriously he helped you, Hamlin, at the moment when you needed help most! And how he boosted Crane and Norris and all the rest of the "young radicals" we thought so wicked in those squeamish days of the early nineties![43]

According to Pattee, intent on shaming his contemporaries into filial respect for Howells, it was a "law" that "no generation ever stands alone; it stands on the shoulders of its fathers and its grandfathers" (p. 113). Although T. S. Eliot had made a very similar claim in "Tradition and the Individual Talent" (1917), the rebellious moderns were not acknowledging, certainly not obeying, this "law."

By the time of Lewis's address, clearly, Howells had entered the twilight zone of literary history where it no longer mattered what he had actually written (as the moderns never read him anyway) or what he really had stood for. His literary reputation was in a total eclipse from which it never fully emerged during the balance of the twentieth century, despite a brief flurry of academic advocacy at mid-century that became known as the "Howells revival."[44]

In 1945, Edwin H. Cady, about to inaugurate his own revisionist biography, contested what by then had become a sacrosanct critical commonplace: "A fashion has arisen in criticism of William Dean Howells of explaining the reticence of his realism, its failure to include lust, terror, and squalor, by suggesting that he failed to face these elements in American life because he was an unconscionable Victorian optimist. . . . Hasty treatment, fortified by the antagonism natural to younger men in revolt against 'The Dean of American Letters,' has led to a tradition unfair to Howells and to a popular misunderstanding of his mind."[45] This "popular misunderstanding" was so entrenched by the 1940s that its original formulation in Brooks (by then a Howells advocate!) had largely been forgotten.[46]

On the mutability of literature and the evanescence of literary reputation, The

Dean himself had said it best in 1902, as he pondered the posthumous decline of Longfellow's stature. He asked Thomas Bailey Aldrich if he had seen "that little new life . . . by a very nice young Columbia professor" who took the fashionable "new view of Longfellow which seems to be composed of his limitations." Yes, the poet had surely been "overrated by the popular love," and it was easy to find fault with him. But Howells felt compelled to write about "the beauty of his art, its refining simplicity without those bounds." This generous impulse produced, in fact, the same "Easy Chair" column that moved Dreiser to declare his own devotion to Howells. "The past obliges," Howells told Aldrich (*SL*, 5:11).

The past obliges.

NOTES

INTRODUCTION

1. Veronica Geng, "My Mao," in *Partners* (New York: Harper and Row, 1984), pp. 17–18, 23. My thanks to Constantine Evans for bringing Geng's essay to my attention.

2. *Selected Letters of W. D. Howells*, ed. George Arms, Christoph K. Lohmann, et al., 6 vols. (Boston: Twayne, 1976–83), 4:45. (Hereafter referred to as *SL*.)

3. Edwin H. Cady, *The Realist at War: The Mature Years, 1885–1920, of William Dean Howells* (Syracuse: Syracuse University Press, 1958), p. 187.

4. "William Dean Howells," *Life* 13 (17 January 1889): 77.

5. William Lyon Phelps, *Essays on Modern Novelists* (New York: Macmillan, 1910), pp. 59–60.

6. Throughout this book I am greatly indebted to *The Realist at War*, which remains, despite its being less than comprehensive, the only satisfactory treatment of Howells's later life. Although there are numerous studies of Howells's earlier career, scholars have typically lost interest in him and his work after 1890. A notorious example is Kenneth Lynn's *William Dean Howells: An American Life* (New York: Harcourt Brace Jovanovich, 1971), the other standard biography, which might more accurately have been subtitled "Half an American Life": Lynn virtually ignores Howells's last three decades.

1. HOWELLS IN 1890

1. Gore Vidal, "William Dean Howells," in *At Home: Essays 1982–1988* (New York: Random House, 1988), p. 164.

2. *Editor's Study by William Dean Howells*, ed. James W. Simpson (Troy, N.Y.: Whitston, 1983), pp. 40–41.

3. W. D. Howells, *Criticism and Fiction* (New York: Harper, 1891), p. 128. The sentence following was also revised to be less *pre*scriptive and more *de*scriptive: "Our novelists, therefore, concern themselves with the more smiling aspects of life, which are the more American, and seek the universal in the individual rather than the social interests."

4. Everett Carter, *Howells and the Age of Realism* (Philadelphia: Lippincott, 1954), p. 180.

5. The lag between composition and publication of the "Editor's Study" was normally

three or four months; the September 1886 column, in which the notorious phrase appeared, had been written in May or June.

6. Howells had received *August Spies' Autobiography; His Speech in Court, and General Notes,* as compiled by Niña Van Zandt, the woman who was married to Spies by proxy while he was in prison. He later read Dyer D. Lum's *Concise History of the Great Trial of the Chicago Anarchists in 1886, Condensed from the Official Record.* A superb modern study is Paul Avrich, *The Haymarket Tragedy* (Princeton: Princeton University Press, 1984).

7. Quoted in Clara M. Kirk and Rudolf Kirk, "William Dean Howells, George William Curtis, and the 'Haymarket Affair,'" *American Literature* 40 (January 1969): 490. After reading the material sent by Howells (Lum's *Concise History*), and sharing it, as Howells had requested, with Charles Eliot Norton, Curtis concluded that "the men are morally responsible for the crime. . . . They are not condemned for their opinions, but for deliberately inciting, without any pretence [*sic*] of reason, to a horrible crime which was committed with disastrous results" (pp. 494–95).

8. Howells's awareness of this constraint was explicit in his letter of 1 December 1887 to William M. Salter, one of the anarchists' chief supporters. Howells regretted that although he wished "not to leave his [Spies's] memory and that of the others to infamy," he could not edit a proposed memorial volume "because my Harper engagement covers all my work. . . . I will contribute a letter—the only form not cut off by my contract" (*SL*, 3:209).

9. Whittier later told an interviewer that Howells had privately begged him to join in "'protesting' against the execution of the Anarchists at Chicago." Howells, upon reading this report, angrily set the record straight: "What I asked you to do was to join me in petitioning the governor to commute the mens' [*sic*] sentence, and in urging you to do this I gave as my reason that I did not think they had been fairly tried" (*SL*, 3:240). In appealing to Whittier, Howells had been strategically careful to delimit his commitment to the anarchists' cause: "The fact is, these men were sentenced for murder when they ought to have been indicted for conspiracy" (*SL*, 3:198).

10. Edwin H. Cady, *The Realist at War: The Mature Years, 1885–1920, of William Dean Howells* (Syracuse: Syracuse University Press, 1958), pp. 77–78. Gore Vidal puts it less charitably: "I suspect that the cautious lifetime careerist advised the Tolstoyan socialist to cool it. Howells was in enough trouble already." But Vidal's praise of "A Word" is justly generous: "As polemic, Howells's letter is more devastating and eloquent than Emile Zola's *J'accuse;* as a defense of the right to express unpopular opinions, it is the equal of what we mistakenly take to be the thrust of Milton's *Areopagitica*" (*At Home,* pp. 166–67).

11. W. D. Howells, "Leo Tolstoi," *Sebastopol* (New York: Harper, 1887), pp. 11, 6, 8. Originally published in *Harper's Weekly* (23 April 1887), this essay was Howells's first extended discussion of Tolstoy, to whom he returned again and again in his "Editor's Study" columns.

12. Howells publicly acknowledged his doubts in his "Editor's Study" of July 1887. Calling Tolstoy "the greatest living writer, and incomparably the greatest writer of fiction who has ever lived," Howells pondered his call to humble toil: "It is a hard saying; but what if it should happen to be the truth? In that case, how many of us who have great

possessions must go away exceeding sorrowful!" After reading *What to Do?*, he concluded, "you cannot be quite the same person you were before; you will be better by taking its truth to heart, or worse by hardening your heart against it" (*Editor's Study*, p. 87).

13. Ibid., p. 129. In the same April 1888 "Editor's Study," Howells also mentioned Richard T. Ely's *Land, Labor and Taxation*. Two months later, he admired Edward Bellamy's *Looking Backward* for its "force of appeal": "whether Mr. Bellamy is amusing himself or not with his conceit of the socialistic state as an accomplished fact, there can be no doubt that he is keenly alive to the defects of our present civilization" (p. 141).

14. Quoted in Cady, *The Realist at War*, p. 90.

15. From a report of the anarchists' meeting, titled "A Letter from W. D. Howells," in the *Chicago Tribune*, 12 November 1888; quoted in Clara Marburg Kirk, *W. D. Howells: Traveler from Altruria, 1889–1894* (New Brunswick: Rutgers University Press, 1962), p. 22. It is likely that the *New York Sun* carried the same story, for Howells's unsent letter of 23 November 1888 was prompted by "the two articles you have printed this week on my 'socialism,' supposed or actual." Neither article has so far been located, but Howells's response suggests that the second was an editorial on the first.

16. Quoted in J. Henry Harper, *The House of Harper: A Century of Publishing in Franklin Square* (New York: Harper, 1912), p. 322.

17. Quoted in Kirk, *W. D. Howells*, p. 19.

18. Quoted in W. D. Howells, *Winifred Howells* (privately printed, 1891), p. 20.

19. On Howells's 1881 breakdown, see John W. Crowley, *The Black Heart's Truth: The Early Career of W. D. Howells* (Chapel Hill: University of North Carolina Press, 1985), pp. 110–46.

20. See Joan Jacobs Brumberg, *Fasting Girls: The Emergence of Anorexia Nervosa as a Modern Disease* (Cambridge, MA: Harvard University Press, 1988). Anorexia nervosa, or hysterical anorexia, was first identified clinically during the 1870s, independently by William Gull in England and Charles Lasègue in France. It is unlikely that Winifred's American physicians were aware of the European medical literature; they consistently diagnosed her illness as hysteria.

21. Quoted in John W. Crowley, *The Mask of Fiction: Essays on W. D. Howells* (Amherst: University of Massachusetts Press, 1989), p. 98.

22. The immediate cause of death was a "heart clot." The relationship, if any, between Winifred's chronic illness and her fatal heart attack cannot be established definitively, but sudden heart failure is sometimes a consequence of anorexia nervosa. For a full discussion of the physical and psychological dimensions of Winifred's case, see Crowley, *The Mask of Fiction*, pp. 83–114.

23. *John Hay—Howells Letters: The Correspondence of John Milton Hay and William Dean Howells, 1861–1905*, ed. George Monteiro and Brenda Murphy (Boston: Twayne, 1980), p. 96.

24. Quoted in Cady, *The Realist at War*, p. 99. On the writing of this novel, see John W. Crowley, "The Unsmiling Aspects of Life: *A Hazard of New Fortunes*," in *Biographies of Books: The Compositional Histories of Notable American Writings*, ed. James Barbour and Tom Quirk (Columbia: University of Missouri Press, 1996).

25. *A Hazard of New Fortunes*, ed. Everett Carter (Bloomington: Indiana University Press, 1976), pp. 4–5. (Hereafter this, the standard edition, is referred to as *HNF*.)

26. *Mark Twain—Howells Letters: The Correspondence of Samuel L. Clemens and William D. Howells, 1872–1910,* ed. Henry Nash Smith and William M. Gibson (Cambridge: Harvard University Press, 1960), p. 603.

27. William Shakespeare, *The Life and Death of King John,* ed. Stanley T. Williams (New Haven: Yale University Press, 1927), pp. 13–14. The best study of the novel in light of its Shakespearean title is Fred G. See, "Howells and the Nature of Fathers," *American Literary Realism* 20 (Spring 1988): 38–54.

28. *Mark Twain—Howells Letters,* pp. 593–94.

29. In a famous passage in *Years of My Youth* (New York: Harper, 1916), Howells wrote: "No man, unless he puts on the mask of fiction, can show his real face or the will behind it" (p. 127). In retrospect, Basil seemed much more like Howells than he had realized when he imagined him: "I too was of the Middle Western birth and growth, and of Bostonian adoption; I had been a journalist as those things went in the simple days of my youth; I had thought myself a poet, and my life was in my literary hopes. I had been all that March was; except an insurance man, and perhaps he never was really an insurance man" (*HNF,* 507).

30. Amy Kaplan, *The Social Construction of American Realism* (Chicago: University of Chicago Press, 1988), p. 61.

31. As Kaplan remarks, "*Hazard* both fulfills and exhausts the project of realism to embrace social diversity within the outlines of a broader community, and to assimilate a plethora of facts and details into a unified narrative form." The disordered ending of *Hazard* "exposes the drive toward moral unity in realism as a dream of mastery to compensate for the lack of control" (*The Social Construction of American Realism,* pp. 62–63).

32. On Howells's youthful vertigo, see Crowley, *The Black Heart's Truth,* pp. 39, 45.

33. See Howells to William Cooper Howells, 20 August 1893 (Houghton Library); Howells to Charles Warren Stoddard, 32 [*sic*] October 1893 (Huntington Library); Howells to Aurelia Howells, 13 January 1895 (Houghton Library). In the August 1893 letter to his father, Howells expressed puzzlement over his malady: "I do not know what brought it on, for I am much stronger than I was last summer, and have apparently a perfect digestion." The reference here to "last summer" implies that vertigo had also afflicted him during the summer of 1892. If so, then the condition was more or less continuous throughout the early 1890s.

34. *My Literary Passions* (New York: Harper, 1895), pp. 86–87. *The Independent Candidate: A Story of To Day* (1854–55) has been reprinted in *The Early Prose Writings of William Dean Howells, 1853–1861,* ed. Thomas Wortham (Athens: Ohio University Press, 1990), pp. 58–98. See also Crowley, *The Black Heart's Truth,* pp. 34–35.

35. *The World of Chance* (New York: Harper, 1893). p. 375. (Hereafter referred to as *WC.*)

36. That *A Modern Romeo* resembles *Geoffrey Winter,* the early (and unpublished) novel that young Howells brought east with him in 1860, is merely one of several striking resemblances between the author and his character. On these parallels, see Scott A. Dennis, "*The World of Chance:* Howells' Hawthornian Self-Parody," *American Literature* 52 (May 1980): 279–93; Sarah B. Daugherty, " 'The Dream of Duty Tormenting Us All': *The World of Chance* and the Decline of Realism," *Harvard Library Bulletin,* n.s., 5 (Spring 1994):

45–52. This apprentice work, under the title *Geoffrey: A Study of American Life,* has now been published by Thomas Wortham in *The Early Prose Writings of William Dean Howells.*

37. As Christopher P. Wilson puts it, in an analysis of the novel in terms of the business of authorship: "*The World of Chance* is something of an intentional un-bildungs-roman—or perhaps, merely the story of another businessman, an artist only by a fiction of the marketplace"; see "Markets and Fictions: Howells' Infernal Juggle," *American Literary Realism* 20 (Spring 1988): 18.

38. Walter Hines Page, in his (anonymous) critique of the publishing industry, cheered the eclipse of "the 'boomed' book, which, having no merit, could once be sold by sheer advertising, in several editions of 100,000 each'" see *A Publisher's Confession* (1905), enl. ed. (Garden City, N.Y.: Doubleday, Page, 1923), p. 18.

39. George N. Bennett, *The Realism of William Dean Howells 1889–1920* (Nashville: Vanderbilt University Press, 1973), p. 52.

40. Dennis, "Howells's Hawthornian Self-Parody," p. 289.

41. On Howells's childhood religious training, see Rodney D. Olsen, *Dancing in Chains: The Youth of William Dean Howells* (New York: New York University Press, 1991).

42. William Alexander, *William Dean Howells: The Realist as Humanist* (New York: Burt Franklin, 1981), p. 129.

2. THE MAN OF LETTERS

1. *Interviews With William Dean Howells,* ed. Ulrich Halfmann (Arlington, Tex.: American Literary Realism, 1973), p. 58.

2. Daniel H. Borus, *Writing Realism: Howells, James, and Norris in the Mass Market* (Chapel Hill: University of North Carolina Press, 1989), p. 40.

3. *Editor's Study by William Dean Howells,* ed. James W. Simpson (Troy, N.Y.: Whitston, 1983), pp. 234–35.

4. Howells's ideas about cultural uplift were widely shared by genteel bookmen during the Gilded Age. The publisher Walter Hines Page, for example, proposed: "We shall both—authors and publishers—get the proper cue if we regard the swarming, eager democracy all about us as a mass of constantly rising men and women, ambitious to grow, with the same higher impulses that we feel in our best moods; and if we interpret our duty as the high privilege of ministering to these higher impulses and not to their lower senses, without commercialism on one side and without academicism on the other, men among men, worthy among the worthy, we may make our calling under such a conception a calling that leads"; see *A Publisher's Confession* (1905), enl. ed. (Garden City, N.Y.: Doubleday, Page, 1923), pp. 175–76.

5. S. S. McClure, *My Autobiography* (1914; repr. New York: Ungar, 1963), p. 235.

6. Borus, *Writing Realism,* p. 49. Edward W. Bok recalled that when his mentor Cyrus Curtis paid $10,000 to serialize *My Literary Passions* in the *Ladies' Home Journal* and then spent another $50,000 advertising the fact, Curtis had explained it was not an expense but an investment: "We are investing in a trade-mark. It will all come back in time"; see *The Americanization of Edward Bok* (1920; repr. New York: Pocket Books, 1965), p. 143. According

to Page, a small general publishing house might budget thirty to fifty thousand dollars for an entire year's outlay on advertising—though some houses spent "a great deal more" (*A Publisher's Confession,* p. 63).

7. By 1895, with both circulation and advertising revenues declining sharply, *Harper's Monthly,* along with the *Atlantic Monthly* and the *Century,* was "losing out to the new *McClure's* magazine, which could be bought at newsstands for fifteen cents a copy compared to their thirty-five cents"; see Eugene Exman, *The House of Harper: One Hundred and Fifty Years of Publishing* (New York: Harper and Row, 1967), p. 180. Nancy Glazener dubs these highbrow magazines "the *Atlantic* group"; see *Reading for Realism: The History of a U.S. Literary Institution, 1850–1910* (Durham: Duke University Press, 1997).

8. Quoted in Clara Marburg Kirk, *W. D. Howells, Traveler From Altruria, 1889–1894* (New Brunswick: Rutgers University Press, 1962), p. 38. Kirk provides the fullest account of Howells's dealings with Walker. For reasons less altogether snobbish than Norton's, Henry James was also appalled when he learned of Howells's contract: "But what, my dear Howells, is the *Cosmopolitan*—why—oh, why (let me not be odious!) are you hanging again round your neck the chain & emblem of bondage? I will be bold enough, at this distance, to tell you that I hate the idea most bitterly, that I hold you too high for such base uses & want you to write only other & yet other American chronicles. *That* is your genius, and not the handling of other people's ineptitudes. I want absolutely to know that there are millions in it; nothing less would satisfy me. Only then, however, the satisfaction would be to know simply that you had refused them. I wish I were nearer & could interfere"; see Michael Anesko, *Letters, Fictions, Lives: Henry James and William Dean Howells* (New York: Oxford University Press, 1997), p. 287.

9. Kirk, *Traveler From Altruria,* pp. 39–40. As Kirk remarks, it was not merely the unexpectedness of Howells's partnership with Walker that occasioned publicity; it was also the symbolic significance of his leap from Boston into the commercial world of New York.

10. In an "Editor's Study" review (March 1891) of Ward McAllister's obsequious tribute to New York's socially elite Four Hundred, Howells remarked: "It is always and everywhere amusing to see a plutocracy trying to turn into an aristocracy. . . . These men who have had no ideal but to get more and more money, these women who have no ideal but to spend more and more, are necessarily ridiculous in the transformation act" (*Editor's Study,* p. 305). Because Walker professed aims higher than conspicuous consumption, Howells may not have taken him to be, strictly speaking, a plutocrat.

11. Christopher P. Wilson, *The Labor of Words: Literary Professionalism in the Progressive Era* (Athens: University of Georgia Press, 1985), p. 8. Early in his career, Howells had enjoyed the sort of political patronage—a consular appointment to Venice—that "had been sought by a remarkably high percentage of American writers prior to 1870" (p. 7).

12. See Jay B. Hubbell, *Who Are the Major American Writers?: A Study of the Changing Literary Canon* (Durham: Duke University Press, 1972), pp. 80–81. Hubbell provides a variety of useful data, taken from nineteenth-century sources, on the relative standing of American authors.

13. Borus, *Writing Realism,* p. 84.

14. It was the usual publishing practice to postdate books that appeared late in a given year. So *Christmas Every Day*, issued on 7 December 1892, bore 1893 on its title page. Only the title story had anything to do with Christmas, although another concerned Thanksgiving. Playing Scrooge in an 1890 "Editor's Study," Howells had humbugged: "The holiday season is upon us with its illustrated books, and again we are reminded of the fact that there seems a demand for inferior quality in all of the arts which superior quality cannot supply" (*Editor's Study*, p. 234).

15. A revised version of the last six "Letters of an Altrurian Traveller" constituted part 1 of *Through the Eye of the Needle* (1907). The complete set of "Letters" in their original serial state did not reappear until 1968, in *The Altrurian Romances*, edited by Clara and Rudolf Kirk for the Indiana Howells Edition.

16. As a result of all these machinations, the order of publication for Howells's longer fictions during the later 1890s scrambled the order of their actual composition, which was *The Story of a Play* (serial 1897, book 1898), *The Day of Their Wedding* (serial 1895, book 1896), *An Open-Eyed Conspiracy* (serial 1896; book 1897), *The Landlord at Lion's Head* (serial 1896, book 1897), and *Ragged Lady* (serial 1898, book 1899).

17. In his autobiography, Edward Bok, editor of the *Ladies' Home Journal*, bragged about the coup of publishing Howells, one of the "two authors of that day [along with Kipling] who commanded more attention than any others." Having surreptitiously bought *The Coast of Bohemia*, Bok withheld announcement of the deal until he had also contracted for *My Literary Passions*: "This surprised the editors of the older magazines, for they realized that the Philadelphia editor had completely tied up the leading novelist of the day for his next two years' output" (*The Americanization of Edward Bok*, pp. 135–36). Bok's claim was obviously exaggerated, but his stretching the truth on this point suggests how important the idea of exclusivity was to him and to the editors he was eager to outstrip.

18. The first fruit of the idea was "Niagara, First and Last," a psychologically revealing account of Howells' reactions to the falls during his 1860 journey. Written either late in 1892 or early in 1893, it became the opening essay in *The Niagara Book: A Complete Souvenir of Niagara Falls* (Buffalo, N.Y.: Underhill and Nichols, 1893).

19. In a 20 August 1893 letter to his father, Howells said he had already finished "My First Visit" and no longer needed him to find the old letters home that might have jogged his memory. In March 1894 Howells sought the advice and approval of Norton and Oliver Wendell Holmes, sending them proof pages of the long essay, the serial text of which would appear in *Harper's Monthly* from May through August 1894.

20. Late in 1893 appeared a musical setting of three of Howells's early poems by Edward MacDowell, probably the leading American composer of the day. This was MacDowell's opus 47, consisting of eight songs with pianoforte accompaniment.

21. Wilson, *The Labor of Words*, p. 41.

22. This preface was old work: from a review in the "Editor's Study" (September 1891) of the first edition of *Main-Travelled Roads*. The new edition was published by Stone and Kimball, which prided itself on the design of its books. Issued before Christmas 1893 in a sumptuous, large-paper format, *Main-Travelled Roads* then appeared in a trade edition early in 1894.

23. See Exman, *The House of Harper*, p. 155.

24. See John J. McCusker, "How Much Is That in Real Money? A Historical Price Index for Use as a Deflator of Money Values in the Economy of the United States," *Proceedings of the American Antiquarian Society* 101, part 2 (1991): 297–333. McCusker's tables, keyed to a composite consumer price index, permit reasonably accurate estimation of relative monetary values. But 1991 is the last year for which McCusker gives any data. Now, nearly a prosperous decade later, Howells's adjusted income figures would be even higher.

25. Edwin H. Cady, *The Realist at War: The Mature Years 1885–1920 of William Dean Howells* (Syracuse: Syracuse University Press, 1958), pp. 192–93. My entire discussion is indebted to Cady's cogent analysis of Howells as a businessman.

By stark contrast, Henry James's income during the 1890s was, on average, less than $3,700 per year, never exceeding $6,000. For all of 1893, James earned $2,923 for his writing, less than a tenth of the $30,000 that Howells counted in March for serial contracts alone; for his own serial rights in 1893, James received a total of $550. See Michael Anesko, *"Friction with the Market": Henry James and the Profession of Authorship* (New York: Oxford University Press, 1986), p. 176.

Consider also the case of Bret Harte, whose sensational popularity during the late 1860s had earned him what (to 1871) was "the most lucrative contract in the history of American literature": a breathtaking offer from the *Atlantic Monthly* of $10,000 for "the exclusive publishing rights to the poems and stories, numbering at least twelve, that he wrote in the course of the coming year." In 1893, Harte's income, mainly from English and American serial rights, was $7,470, an amount that equals his average earnings from 1890 to 1899, with no single year in excess of $11,000. This average amount is also equivalent, in deflated 1893 dollars, to the $10,000 contract of 1871. See Nils Axel Nissen, *Prince and Pauper: The Life and Literary Career of Bret Harte* (Oslo, Norway: University of Oslo, 1996), pp. 33, 275.

26. In June 1891 Howells wrangled with Henry Mills Alden over royalties from *The Quality of Mercy*, for which the Harpers were proposing to pay the earlier, lower rate because the novel predated their new contract with Howells. He argued vehemently that the choice to write his *Sun* novel before the one he owed the Harpers "was made in their interest, of which I have always been as observant as of my own; for I foresaw that otherwise the two serials would be running simultaneously. . . . I think that in view of all the circumstances they should pay me 20 per cent. on all copies, cloth and paper alike, of the *Sun* story" (*SL*, 3:313). Franklin Square capitulated, saving face by agreeing to pay only 10 percent on the paper edition.

27. This economically advantageous practice—used by Irving, Cooper, and Longfellow earlier in the century—was feasible only for a firmly established writer with plenty of capital to invest in his own career. During the 1890s, only best-selling authors could demand twenty percent and *not* provide the plates. Page deplored such high royalites as "ruinous" of publishers' fiscal stability and ultimately damaging to authors as well; see *A Publisher's Confession*, pp. 3–23.

28. Borus, *Writing Realism*, p. 50.

29. Frank Norris, "Fiction Writing as a Business," in *The Responsibilities of the Novelist* (1903; repr. New York: Hill and Wang, 1967), pp. 258–59. Norris remarks, however, that few writers ever exploit the system so thoroughly. On the contrary, most make a pittance in a literary market where 2,500 copies is an extraordinary sale for a novel, but one that yields only $250—or, roughly, $2.50 a day—from the standard 10 percent royalty on books. "An expert carpenter will easily make twice that, and the carpenter has infinitely the best of it in that he can keep the work up year in and year out, where the novelist must wait for a new idea, and the novel writer must then jockey and manoeuvre for publication" (p. 256).

30. Borus, *Writing Realism,* p. 41.

31. "The Man of Letters as a Man of Business" (1893), in *Literature and Life,* Library Edition (New York: Harper, 1911), p. 7. (Hereafter referred to as *ML*).

32. According to Borus, the standard rate at the quality magazines during the 1890s was 3/4 of a cent per word (1/2 a cent for unknowns); Crane was earning 3 cents a word while Howells was getting 10 cents (*Writing Realism,* p. 43).

33. Page estimated that there were, "perhaps, a dozen American novelists who have large incomes from their work; there are many more who have comfortable incomes; but there is none whose income is as large as the writers of gossip for the literary journals would have us believe." Howells, whose income was certainly "comfortable," was nevertheless not among the wealthiest writers: "It is a hard world in which 'Knighthood,' 'Quincy Adams Sawyer' and 'Graustark,' to say nothing of 'The One Woman,' 'Alice of Old Vincennes' and a hundred more 'poor' books make fortunes, while Mr. Howells and Mr. James write to unresponsive markets and even Mr. Kipling cannot find so many readers for a new novel as Mr. Bacheller of 'Eben Holden' " (*A Publisher's Confession,* pp. 21–22, 28).

34. Cady, *The Realist at War,* p. 195.

35. Wilson, *The Labor of Words,* p. 11.

36. Richard Ohmann, *Politics of Letters* (Middletown, Conn.: Wesleyan University Press, 1987), pp. 26, 28, 143.

37. *Editor's Study,* pp. 243–44.

38. Ibid., p. 313.

39. Alan Trachtenberg, *The Incorporation of America: Culture and Society in the Gilded Age* (New York: Hill and Wang, 1982), p. 196. Howells told Howard Pyle that although he saw "nothing final or hopeful" in the status of artists and artisans, he believed that they had "cleaner hands than any other kind of people, and may well be content without cake as long as they have bread"; see *Life in Letters of William Dean Howells,* ed. Mildred Howells (Garden City, N.Y.: Doubleday, Doran, 1928), 2:40.

40. Borus, *Writing Realism,* p. 66.

41. Lewis P. Simpson, "The Treason of William Dean Howells," in *The Man of Letters in New England and the South: Essays on the History of the Literary Vocation in America* (Baton Rouge: Louisiana State University Press, 1973), pp. 91–92. Simpson's brilliant essay, written long before the literary marketplace became a vogue of new-style cultural studies, has been formative of my thinking on these matters.

42. Howard Pyle, for one, was evidently confused by Howells's tone in "The Man of Letters as a Man of Business." Howells was perplexed by Pyle's reaction: "I don't quite know what you find dim or uncertain in my Scribner paper, for I fancied it very outright as to the irony and the earnest, so that one could not well be mistaken for the other" (*Life in Letters,* 2:40).

43. In 1891, Bok bid $6,000 for Mark Twain's *The American Claimant* but ultimately lost the book to McClure at double the price. John Brisben Walker was also paying top dollar for anything, however feeble, Mark Twain would give him for *Cosmopolitan*—such as $800 for "The Esquimau Maiden's Romance." Clemens took an instant dislike to Walker, he told Howells, but he was still happy enough to take his money. See *Mark Twain—Howells Letters: The Correspondence of Samuel L. Clemens and William D. Howells, 1872–1910,* ed. Henry Nash Smith and William M. Gibson (Cambridge: Harvard University Press, 1960), pp. 644 n, 652 n.

3. THE MAKING OF "THE DEAN"

1. J. Henry Harper, *The House of Harper: A Century of Publishing in Franklin Square* (New York: Harper, 1912), p. 323.

2. Two months after "The Man of Letters as a Man of Business" had appeared in *Scribner's,* the magazine begged to differ editorially with a passing remark of Howells: "to the effect that magazines, however much they might enrich writers, crowded out 'pure literature' with their typical mixture of 'two-thirds popular science, politics, economics, and the timely topics which I will call contemporanics,' and consequently had the effect of narrowing the field of literary activity." On the contrary, the *Scribner's* editor argued, the problem was a dearth of distinguished literary submissions; and he challenged Howells to name a single writer who had been "rejected solely on the grounds that space was lacking for pure literature." In Howells's own case, furthermore, "the magazine doubted his work had ever been limited by the pages given over to, say, popular science"; see Ronald Weber, *Hired Pens: Professional Writers in America's Golden Age of Print* (Athens: Ohio University Press, 1997), pp. 249–50. This exchange seems to support Howells's inference that an alleged lack of space in the Harper magazines was a cover story for editorial reservations about the quality of his (purely literary) work.

3. *If Not Literature: Letters of Elinor Howells,* ed. Ginette de B. Merrill and George Arms (Columbus: Ohio State University Press, 1988), p. 275.

4. Edwin H. Cady, *The Realist at War: The Mature Years 1885–1920 of William Dean Howells* (Syracuse: Syracuse University Press, 1958), p. 223.

5. See G. Ferris Chronkhite, "Howells Turns to the Inner Life," *New England Quarterly* 30 (December 1957): 474–85. My own studies of Howells' late psychological fiction are found in *The Mask of Fiction: Essays on W. D. Howells* (Amherst: University of Massachusetts Press, 1989).

6. Eugene Exman, *The House of Harper: One Hundred and Fifty Years of Publishing* (New York: Harper and Row, 1967), p. 181. During the summer of 1899, when Harper and Brothers defaulted on loans to Morgan's bank, the firm had been forcibly reorganized

under the leadership of S. S. McClure. But McClure then fell short of raising the capital necessary to buy out the house; after he withdrew, in October 1899, Harvey took over as the choice of both debtor and creditor.

7. Harper, *The House of Harper*, p. 325.

8. George C. Carrington Jr., introduction to *The Kentons* (Bloomington: Indiana University Press, 1971), p. xxiii. Carrington gives a full account of the production and reception of this novel.

9. Harper, *The House of Harper*, p. 326.

10. Howells to Aurelia Howells, 13 July 1902; quoted in Cady, *The Realist at War*, p. 194. Cady suggests ten thousand copies as a median figure for Howells's typical sales. Howells noted in 1902 that *A Modern Instance* had taken a decade to sell ten thousand (*SL*, 5:26).

11. Daniel Borus, *Writing Realism: Howells, James, and Norris in the Mass Market* (Chapel Hill: University of North Carolina Press, 1989), p. 118.

12. "The Man of Letters as a Man of Business," in *Literature and Life*, Library Edition (New York: Harper, 1911), p. 4.

13. James B. Pond, *Eccentricities of Genius: Memories of Famous Men and Women of the Platform and Stage* (New York: Dillingham, 1900), p. 333. Pond stated bluntly that he had pursued the elusive Howells as a client mainly because of Mark Twain's insistence: "and on that recommendation, more than my love for his books, few of which I have ever read, I have used my persuasive eloquence on him more than on any other American author" (p. 333). So small was Pond's familiarity with Howells, in fact, that he commissioned George W. Cable to write a few panegyrical pages to pad out the Major's scant account of Howells' career.

14. Howells's standard performance consisted of his reading from the prepared text of "Novel-Writing and Novel-Reading." For the 1899 tour, however, he worked up an alternate lecture, titled "Heroes and Heroines of Fiction," which proved to be so unsuccessful in the field that he quickly dropped it (although it was later greatly expanded into the 1901 *Heroines of Fiction*).

15. *Mark Twain—Howells Letters: The Correspondence of Samuel L. Clemens and William D. Howells, 1872–1910*, ed. Henry Nash Smith and William M. Gibson (Cambridge: Harvard University Press, 1960), p. 700.

16. Mark Twain's letter to Pond echoed the cynical stranger's curse in the recently published story, "The Man That Corrupted Hadleyburg": "Go, and reform—or, mark my words — some day, for your sins, you will die and go to hell or Hadleyburg—TRY AND MAKE IT THE FORMER"; see *The Man That Corrupted Hadleyburg and Other Stories and Essays* (New York: Harper, 1900), p. 47. During Howells's tour, Clemens consolingly wrote to him: "Oh, *I* know how you feel! I've been in hell myself. You are there tonight. By difference in time you are at luncheon, now—& not eating it. Nothing is so loathsome as gadding around platforming" (*Mark Twain—Howells Letters*, p. 710).

17. Richard Brodhead points out that "popular" was redefined during the later nineteenth century to denote "not just 'well-liked' or 'widely read' but specifically production *into* a certain market status through commercial management of a book's [or an author's] public life." Mass entertainment, of which the lecture circuit was one flourishing form,

produced spectators who consumed voyeuristically and passively; it "held its audience in the position *of* audience by seeming to embody consumable 'life' "; see "Veiled Ladies: Toward a History of Antebellum Entertainment," *American Literary History* 1 (Summer 1989): 280, 285.

18. *Mark Twain—Howells Letters,* p. 712.

19. *Life in Letters of William Dean Howells,* ed. Mildred Howells (Garden City, N.Y.: Doubleday, Doran, 1928), 2:77.

20. Howells acknowledged to Clemens that despite all its problems, lecturing had definitely been lucrative: "I made at least half as much money as Pond promised, so that the thing remains a temptation as well as a horror" (*Mark Twain—Howells Letters,* p. 713).

21. Robert Rowlette, "William D. Howells' 1899 Midwest Lecture Tour," *American Literary Realism* 9 (Winter 1976): 1–2. See also "In 'The Silken Arms of the Aristocracy': William Dean Howells' Lecture in Indianapolis, 1899," *Indiana Magazine of History* 69 (December 1973): 299–319; "William D. Howells' 1899 Midwest Lecture Tour" [part 2], *American Literary Realism* 10 (Spring 1977): 125–67. Rowlette's accounts have been supplemented and slightly corrected in Thomas Wortham, "W. D. Howells' 1899 Midwest Lecture Tour: What the Letters Tell," *American Literary Realism* 11 (Autumn 1978): 265–74.

22. Cady, *The Realist at War,* p. 223.

23. Rowlette, "William D. Howells' 1899 Midwest Lecture Tour," pp. 13, 14, 17.

24. Quoted in Clayton L. Eichelberger, *Published Comment on William Dean Howells Through 1920: A Research Bibliography* (Boston: G. K. Hall, 1976), pp. 193–94. Eichelberger's invaluable work has greatly assisted my exploration of The Dean's evolution. The book of poems mentioned in the ad must have been *Stops of Various Quills* (1895).

25. Gerald Stanley Lee, "Mr. Howells on the Platform" (1899); repr. in *Critical Essays on W. D. Howells, 1866–1920,* ed. Edwin H. Cady and Norma W. Cady (Boston: G. K. Hall, 1983), pp. 193–94.

26. Nathanael West, *Miss Lonelyhearts and The Day of the Locust* (New York: New Directions, 1969), pp. 13–14.

27. Ibid., p. 14

28. The classic, though controversial, study is Ann Douglas, *The Feminization of American Culture* (New York: Knopf, 1977). Douglas' book does not deal directly with the later nineteenth century; for an extension of her approach to Howells and James, see Alfred Habegger, *Gender, Fantasy, and Realism in American Literature* (New York: Columbia University Press, 1982).

29. When the *Critic* invited his readers in 1884 to nominate "Our Forty Immortals" for a hypothetical American Academy, Howells placed fifth—behind Holmes, Lowell, Whittier, and Bancroft, but well ahead of Henry James and Mark Twain (thirteenth and fourteenth respectively). In 1904, when the American Academy of Arts and Letters became a reality, Howells was first among the seven charter members; and he was later elected president of the academy, an office he held until his death.

30. Cather's name appeared in its triple-barreled form on the title pages of all her early novels through *My Ántonia* (1918); she became plain "Willa Cather" after switching from the old-fashioned Boston house of Houghton Mifflin Company to Alfred A. Knopf, the

brilliant New York publisher who was gaining a reputation for his list of sophisticated books by the rising moderns. In this company, "Willa Sibert Cather" would have been quite incongruous. West's pun on Cather/catheter—with its strong overtones of phallic anxiety—recalls Ernest Hemingway's vicious letter to Edmund Wilson jeering *One of Ours* (1922), Cather's Pulitzer Prize novel about World War I. "Wasn't that last scene in the lines wonderful?" he scoffed. "Do you know where it came from? The battle scene in *Birth of a Nation.* I identified episode after episode, Catherized. Poor woman she had to get her war experience somewhere"; see *Ernest Hemingway: Selected Letters, 1917–1961,* ed. Carlos Baker (New York: Scribner, 1981), p. 105.

31. "Bartleby, The Scrivener: A Story of Wall-Street," in *Herman Melville* (New York: Library of America, 1984), p. 636.

32. F. Scott Fitzgerald, *The Great Gatsby* (1925; repr. New York: Scribner, 1953), p. 120. The triple-barreled name was differentially gendered. For a woman who married, the use of a middle "maiden" name publicly marked her transfer from a father's to a husband's house. Unmarried women who used three names, such as Jewett and Cather, could easily have been (mis)read as being married. The use of three names for men, the declaration of whose marital status was less imperative than for women, seems mainly to have signified a certain degree of formality, implying upper-class rank or greater substance, material or otherwise.

33. Because Howells planned to append "Niagara Revisited" to a new edition of *Their Wedding Journey,* he did not want his copyright to be compromised. So he filed suit against the Chicago publisher, and the edition was suppressed. As a result of this swift injunction, less than a dozen copies of *Niagara Revisited* have survived, making it Howells's rarest title for collectors.

34. I own, for example, a small card, of the type designed for collecting autographs, that "W. D. Howells" signed on 13 January 1876, during his reign as *Atlantic* editor.

35. Edwin Bok, *The Americanization of Edward Bok* (1920; repr. New York: Pocket Books, 1965), pp. 152–53.

36. *Life in Letters,* 2:127–28. Howells passed on the gift vase to Aurelia.

37. As early as 1897, Albert Lee published "A Bibliography of the First Editions of the Writings of W. D. Howells" in the *Book Buyer;* but the trade in Howells first editions has never really thrived. An 1899 auction in New York, which coincided with his midwestern lecture tour, reportedly fell below expectations, attracting "little attention and low bids" (see Eichelberger, *William Dean Howells,* p. 209). Antiquarian book dealers will tell you that things have not improved much since then. In one standard price guide, the rare *Poems of Two Friends* (1860) is one of a very few titles whose value has stagnated (at about $750) in a consistently rising market for "first books." The going price of an author's first book generally sets the upper limit for everything else; and except for one or two rarities, Howells' first editions currently sell for a fraction of Mark Twain's, well below Henry James's or Stephen Crane's, a little below Edith Wharton's, about on par with Sarah Orne Jewett's, but above Hamlin Garland's. It should be noted, however, that a large and unusually comprehensive Howells collection—more than 350 books as well as other Howellsiana—was recently placed on the market for $70,000.

38. Of all Howells's books, *Venetian Life* was the one most often reprinted, in a wide variety of formats, including gift editions. As early as 1885, it appeared in two volumes in the elegant Riverside Aldine series. In 1892, a more extravagant two-volume edition featured tipped-in watercolor illustrations by Childe Hassam and other notable artists. As James Woodress says, "At the age of seventy Howells was still drawing royalties from *Venetian Life*, first published when he was twenty-nine." The 1907 edition was prompted, in fact, by economic considerations: copyright was about to expire. To keep the royalties flowing, Howells added a new introduction and conclusion and touched up the book internally so as to qualify it for renewed protection; see "*Venetian Life:* Background, Composition, Publication, and Reception," *The Old Northwest* 8 (Spring 1982): 61–62.

39. Michael Anesko, *Letters, Fictions, Lives: Henry James and William Dean Howells* (New York: Oxford University Press, 1997), pp. 331–39. I am generally indebted to Anesko's analysis.

40. Quoted in Anesko, *Letters, Fictions, Lives*, pp. 334, 335. Mifflin's rancor over Howells's defection reflects the conviction of conservative publishers that writers who switched houses were breaking the gentlemen's agreement that regulated the book trade—in part, by proscribing competitive bidding for the services of popular authors. As Walter Hines Page wrote, "It was once a matter of honor that one publisher should respect the relation established between another publisher and a writer, as a physician respects the relation established between another physician and a patient. Three or four of the best publishing houses still live and work by this code"; see *A Publisher's Confession* (1905), enl. ed. (Garden City, N.Y.: Doubleday, Page, 1923), p. 65.

41. Anesko, *Letters, Fictions, Lives*, pp. 335, 336, 334.

42. Michael Anesko, "The Road to Whited Sepulchre," working paper for the 1996 Howells Conference at Kittery Point, Maine.

43. For several years Howells had been blowing hot and cold about writing a biography of James Russell Lowell; and in this letter to Norton (Lowell's literary executor), he seemed to be suggesting a deal by which he might do the biography for Houghton Mifflin in exchange for their cooperation in a Harper Library Edition. But Howells later came to the conclusion that he was written out on Lowell and could not produce a biography.

44. As Anesko points out in *Letters, Fictions, Lives*, Howells' publishers had never really overcome their differences, although they led him to believe otherwise. In issuing the first six volumes without consultation, Harper and Brothers irrevocably annoyed Houghton Mifflin; no further cooperation was possible.

45. *Editor's Study by William Dean Howells*, ed. James W. Simpson (Troy, N.Y.: Whitston, 1983), p. 236.

46. H. L. Mencken, "The Dean" (1919), in Cady and Cady, *Critical Essays on W. D. Howells*, p. 260.

4. THE AGE OF HOWELLS

1. It is not clear whether this letter was actually read at the Tolstoy dinner before it was published in the *Critic* (October 1898). Howells told Stedman that the kind gesture had touched him deeply (*SL*, 4:213).

2. Stedman's canon did not withstand the modernist wave. By 1919, the prolific anthologist Louis Untermeyer (who was himself to be satirized by e. e. cummings) could flippantly dismiss *An American Anthology* as a "gargantuan collection of mediocrity and moralizing" that contained "perhaps sixty pages of genuine poetry and no more than ten pages of what might be called American poetry"; quoted in Jay B. Hubbell, *Who Are the Major American Writers? A Study of the Changing Literary Canon* (Durham: Duke University Press, 1972), p. 100.

3. *Editor's Study by William Dean Howells,* ed. James W. Simpson (Troy, N.Y.: Whitston, 1983), p. 361.

4. *The Letters of Edith Wharton,* ed. R. W. B. Lewis and Nancy Lewis (New York: Scribner, 1988), p. 62.

5. John A. Macy, *The Spirit of American Literature* (1913; repr. New York: Boni and Liveright, 1923), p. 281.

6. *Editor's Study,* pp. 245–46.

7. One name that could *not* have come to mind was Emily Dickinson, whom Howells had yet to read. But when he reviewed the first volume of Dickinson's posthumously published poetry in the "Editor's Study" for January 1891, he immediately recognized her significance for American literary history: "If nothing else had come out of our life but this strange poetry we should feel that in the work of Emily Dickinson America, or New England rather, had made a distinctive addition to the literature of the world, and could not be left out of any record of it; and the interesting and important thing is that this poetry is as characteristic of our life as our business enterprise, our political turmoil, our demagogism, our millionairism" (*Editor's Study,* p. 296).

8. See Van Wyck Brooks, "America's Coming of Age" (1915), in *Three Essays on America,* ed. James R. Vitelli (New York: Dutton, 1970). Brooks's highbrow/lowbrow formulation, which derived from George Santayana's famous 1911 address on "The Genteel Tradition in American Philosophy," in turn influenced Philip Rahv's division of American writers into "palefaces" and "redskins." See *The Genteel Tradition: Nine Essays by George Santayana,* ed. Douglas L. Wilson (Cambridge: Harvard University Press, 1967); Philip Rahv, "Paleface and Redskin" (1939), in *Essays on Literature and Politics, 1932–1972,* ed. Arabel J. Porter and Andrew J. Dvosin (Boston: Houghton Mifflin, 1978), pp. 3–7.

9. *Editor's Study,* pp. 342–43.

10. David R. Shumway, *Creating American Civilization: A Genealogy of American Literature as an Academic Discipline* (Minneapolis: University of Minnesota Press, 1994), pp. 26, 49.

11. Richard Ohmann, *Politics of Letters* (Middletown, Conn.: Wesleyan University Press, 1987), p. 32. Ohmann centers his analysis on "the year 1893, plus or minus one" (p. 26). See chapter 2 for my treatment of Howells's career during the exactly same period.

12. William James, "The Ph.D. Octopus" (1903), in *Memories and Studies* (New York: Longmans, Green, 1911), p. 343.

13. Howells himself entered this market with *Stories of Ohio* (1897), a set of historical adventure narratives aimed at schoolchildren, published by the American Book Company, a leading purveyor of textbooks. Howells was released for this project from his exclusive contract with Harper and Brothers, which had not yet entered the schoolbook

field. See Eugene L. Pattison, "Ambiguities in History: The Making of *Stories of Ohio, The Old Northwest* 8 (Summer 1982): 101–17.

14. Shumway, *Creating American Civilization,* pp. 60, 126.

15. Nina Baym, "Early Histories of American Literature: A Chapter in the Institution of New England," *American Literary History* 1 (Fall 1989): 471. Poe and Whitman were anomalous figures in the textbooks—as they were for Howells—because they complicated the Whig historical project of locating American culture in the Anglo-Saxon heritage of New England.

16. Milan Kundera, *The Art of the Novel* (New York: Grove, 1988), p. 133.

17. "The interview is an invention of American journalism, and is credited, or discredited, to J. B. McCullagh." The genre was apparently flourishing in New York newspapers by 1869, when the *London Daily News* sniffed that some American dailies were "bringing the profession of journalism into contempt, so far as they can, by a kind of toadyism or flunkeyism which they call 'interviewing.' " See Silas Bent, *Ballyhoo: The Voice of the Press* (New York: Boni and Liveright, 1927), p. 104. See also Nils Gunnar Nilsson, "The Origin of the Interview," *Journalism Quarterly* 48 (1971): 707–13.

18. *Life in Letters of William Dean Howells,* ed. Mildred Howells (Garden City, N.Y.: Doubleday, Doran, 1928), 2:59–60.

19. See Ginette de B. Merrill and George Arms, "Howells at Belmont: The Case of the 'Wicked Interviewer,' " *Harvard Library Bulletin* 30 (April 1982): 153–78.

20. Daniel H, Borus, *Writing Realism: Howells, James, and Norris in the Mass Market* (Chapel Hill: University of North Carolina Press, 1989), p. 125. Howells's first newspaper interview, with a reporter from the *Baltimore American and Commercial Advertiser* in October 1883, is listed in Clayton L. Eichelberger, *Published Comment on William Dean Howells Through 1920: A Research Bibliography* (Boston: G. K. Hall, 1976), p. 43. See also *Interviews With William Dean Howells,* ed. Ulrich Halfmann (Arlington, Tex.: American Literary Realism, 1973). The earliest interview collected by Halfmann dates from 1886; the majority were given during or after Howells's 1899 lecture tour.

21. *Interviews,* p. 57.

22. *Mark Twain—Howells Letters,* p. 732.

23. Edwin H. Cady, *The Realist at War: The Mature Years, 1885–1920, of William Dean Howells* (Syracuse: Syracuse University Press, 1958), p. 205. Other quotations are identified in the text.

24. *Interviews,* p. 45.

25. Ulrich Halfmann, "Dreiser and Howells: New Light on Their Relationship," *Amerikastudien* 20 (1975): 73.

26. *Interviews,* p. 59. "How He Climbed Fame's Ladder" was reprinted under different titles in two collections of inspirational literature edited by the publisher of *Success,* Orison Swett Marden: "How William Dean Howells Worked to Secure a Foothold," in *How They Succeeded; Life Stories of Successful Men Told by Themselves* (Boston: Lothrop, 1901); and "A Printer's Boy, Self-Taught, Becomes the Dean of American Letters," in *Little Visits With Great Americans; or, Success Ideals and How to Attain Them* (New York: Success Company, 1903).

The "Dean of American Letters" appears nowhere in the interview itself. That it was added to the title in 1903 suggests the growing familiarity with this term.

27. In view of the fraudulent 1898 interview, Edwin H. Cady and Norma W. Cady argue that "nothing Dreiser ever said about Howells is to be credited in the absence of evidence external to Dreiser. Where is the document to show that Howells ever made an appointment with Dreiser? Lacking such evidence, Dreiser's 'second interview' with Howells becomes as suspect as the 'first' "; see *Critical Essays on W. D. Howells, 1866–1920,* ed. Edwin H. Cady and Norma W. Cady (Boston: G. K. Hall, 1983), p. xxviii. To my knowledge there is no such proof that the second interview occurred, and the extreme skepticism of the Cadys may, in fact, be warranted (although their perspective on the Howells-Dreiser relationship seems unduly hostile toward Dreiser).

28. *Interviews,* p. 67. The sobriquet may be said to have become official two years later, when Howells's old friend and Tolstoyan comrade, Edward Everett Hale, published a review titled "The Dean of American Letters" in the *Dial* 33 (16 November 1902): 323–24.

29. *Interviews,* p. 69.

30. When Howells first met Carnegie in 1892, he told his father that although he liked him somehow, he would nevertheless "rather not be one of his hands" (*SL,* 4:12). In April 1903, Howells described for Norton his first impressions of Carnegie's New York home, after a party there for a visiting English dignitary. Howells was favorably impressed, particularly by Carnegie's recent offer to cover the $40 million owed by Venezuela to European claimants, in order to forestall hostilities: "I sat on Carnegie's left, and had moments of confidence with him in which I could tell him of my pleasure in his offer to buy off a war by paying the debts of a nation. He is a dreamer and in his way a poet, and he seemed to like my notion that this was a stroke of poetry. I found both him and his wife simple-hearted and quite unspoiled. . . . The house is subjectively rather than objectively rich, and outside is a triumph of ugliness, though within it is very home-like" (*SL,* 5:50).

31. Ellen Moers, *Two Dreisers* (New York: Viking, 1969), p. 44.

32. Cady, *The Realist at War,* p. 208. For Cady's detailed discussion of Howells's relationships to younger writers, see pp. 208–22. Cady also cites the amusing instance of the aspirant who threatened the *Century:* "If you do not take some of my contributions, I shall have to resort to the humiliation of being discovered by William Dean Howells" (p. 210).

33. See William L. Andrews, "William Dean Howells and Charles W. Chesnutt: Criticism and Race Fiction in the Age of Booker T. Washington," in *On Howells: The Best from American Literature,* ed. Edwin H. Cady and Louis J. Budd (Durham: Duke University Press, 1993); and Joanne B. Karpinski, "When the Marriage of True Minds Admits Impediments: Charlotte Perkins Gilman and William Dean Howells," in *Patrons and Protégés: Gender, Friendship, and Writing in Nineteenth-Century America,* ed. Shirley Marchalonis (New Brunswick: Rutgers University Press, 1988). For a less jaundiced view of the latter relationship, see Julie Bates Dock, et al., " 'But One Expects That': Charlotte Perkins Gilman's 'The Yellow Wallpaper' and the Shifting Light of Scholarship," *PMLA* 111 (1996): 52–65.

34. "What Is Dirt?" *Bookman* 70 (November 1929): 258–62; "What Is Happening to Our Fiction," *Nation* 129 (4 December 1929): 673–74; quoted in Louis J. Budd, *Robert Herrick* (New York: Twayne, 1971), p. 102. Hemingway was so badly stung by Herrick's attack that he threatened the *Bookman*'s editor "with a physical spanking for having printed such trash." See Carlos Baker, *Ernest Hemingway: A Life Story* (New York: Scribner, 1969), p. 206.

35. "The Novels of Robert Herrick," *North American Review* 189 (June 1909); repr. in W. D. Howells, *Selected Literary Criticism, vol. 3, 1898–1920,* ed. Ronald Gottesman (Bloomington: Indiana University Press, 1993), pp. 132–133. Herrick was grateful for Howells' review as "almost the first work of authoritative criticism, of *understanding* appreciation" his fiction had received (*SL,* 5:268 n). Budd calls the review a "milestone in [the] growth of Herrick's contemporary reputation" (*Robert Herrick,* p. 137).

36. Moers, *Two Dreisers,* p. 44.

37. *Interviews,* p. 69. Dreiser does not identify the "struggler" in the interview itself; that he was referring to himself is suggested by Moers, *Two Dreisers,* p. 44.

38. Robert H. Elias, *Theodore Dreiser: Apostle of Nature,* emended edition (Ithaca: Cornell University Press, 1970), p. 95. Elias reports rumors circulating in August 1898 that Dodd, Mead, and Company was about to publish a book of Dreiser's poetry, partly on Howells's strong recommendation. If so, it is not clear if, how, and when Dreiser came into personal contact with Howells. In the second interview, written during 1899, Dreiser speaks of passing Howells on the street one January day, and then of dropping in at his apartment sometime later for an impromptu interview. Although Dreiser strongly implies further familiarity with Howells, he never actually claims that another face-to-face meeting took place. The implication, which is confirmed by Halfmann's findings about the faked 1898 interview, is that if Howells indeed had read Dreiser's poetry before early 1900, he must have done so at Dreiser's written request. That is, Dreiser did not likely arrive at Howells's apartment (if he ever did!) literally with his verses in hand. Although one must be wary of drawing any firm conclusions from Dreiser's own accounts of his dealings with Howells, it seems too incredible that Dreiser made up every detail. More likely, the two men met and talked, possibly more than once, and Dreiser then "improved" on the actual circumstances, in part to enlarge his own stature.

39. Dreiser to Howells, 14 May 1902; in Moers, *Two Dreisers,* pp. 175–76.

40. Ibid., p. 176.

41. As Halfmann suggests, Dreiser may have been largely unfamiliar with Howells's work beyond a few recent items. He certainly was ignorant of Howells's repeated attention to Hardy: "In reality, by 1902 Howells had reviewed four of Hardy's novels as well as his poems and a dramatization of *Tess of the d'Urbervilles,* had praised him in several interviews, included him among his *Literary Passions,* and devoted two chapters to his heroines in the second volume of *Heroines of Fiction*" ("Dreiser and Howells," p. 83). See also Elsa Nettels, "Howells and Hardy," *Colby Library Quarterly* 20 (June 1984): 107–22.

42. *Interviews,* p. 69.

43. Halfmann attributes the problem to the fraudulence of the 1898 interview: "the crucial first contact with Dreiser which created in Howells deep-rooted mental and

temperamental reservations about his 'interviewer'—reservations which (although he received Dreiser at his home for the *Ainslee's* interview in 1899) increased in the years to follow" ("Dreiser and Howells," p. 82). Given their clashing personalities, I suspect that the slick, florid, and egocentric young Dreiser would not have had to do anything dishonest in order to inspire Howells's instant and intuitive dislike.

44. Dorothy Dudley, *Dreiser and the Land of the Free* (New York: Beechhurst, 1946), p. 197. Dreiser himself was Dudley's only source on Howells's reaction to *Sister Carrie;* however, under the painful circumstances, it is entirely possible that Dreiser would have remembered Howells's exact words to him.

45. Halfmann points out that Howells never mentioned Dreiser in hundreds of magazine pieces he published between 1900 and 1920: he neither reviewed any of his several books nor referred to him in any interview with another reporter. There was, moreover, nothing said in "the thousands of Howells letters of the same period, published or unpublished," except for one oblique reference to *The "Genius"*—and, presumably, the lost reply to Dreiser's letter in 1902 ("Dreiser and Howells," p. 81).

46. Elias points to the extremely wide base of support, nearly five hundred persons, from conservatives to Greenwich Village radicals: "Ultimately the advocates of Dreiser's rights ranged from James Lane Allen and Mary E. Wilkins Freeman to Jack London and Sinclair Lewis, from Edwin Arlington Robinson and Willa Cather to Gelett Burgess and James Oliver Curwood, from Ellery Sedgwick and Willam Allen White to Max Eastman and John Reed, and included names as various as David Belasco, James Montgomery Flagg, William Gillette, Percy Stickney Grant, Adachi Kinnosuke, and David S. Muzzey" (*Theodore Dreiser,* p. 201).

47. Dudley, *Dreiser and the Land of the Free,* pp. 115, 143.

48. *The Letters of Edith Wharton,* p. 369.

49. R. W. B. Lewis, *Edith Wharton: A Biography* (New York: Harper and Row, 1975), p. 116.

50. When Howells twitted Henry James in 1902 about a hotel in New York being renamed in his honor, James replied: "The Henry James, I opine, will be a terrifically 'private' hotel. . . . Refined, liveried, 'two-toileted,' it will have been a short-lived hectic paradox, or will presently have to close in order to reopen as the Mary Johnson [*sic*] or the K. W. Wiggin [*sic*] or the James Lane Allen. Best of all as the Edith Wharton" (*SL,* 5:12 n). By placing Wharton in the disreputable company of such best-selling romancers as Mary Johnston, Kate Douglas Wiggin, and James Lane Allen, James implied his own reservations about her talent at this early point in her career. It may be, in fact, that Howells' sense of Wharton's undue indebtedness to James came from James himself.

51. *The Letters of Edith Wharton,* p. 287. "Doyen" comes from the same root as "dean": *decanus.*

52. Ibid., pp. 290, 293–94.

53. Lewis, *Edith Wharton,* p. 340.

54. Wharton to Lewis, 9 February 1931; quoted in Ellen Phillips DuPree, "Wharton, Lewis and the Nobel Prize Address," *American Literature* 56 (May 1984): 265.

55. Edith Wharton, *A Backward Glance* (New York: Appleton-Century, 1934), p. 148.

56. Harriet Waters Preston, "The Latest Novels of Howells and James," *Atlantic Monthly*

91 (January 1903); repr. in *The War of the Critics over William Dean Howells,* ed. Edwin H. Cady and David L. Frazier (Evanston, Ill. and Elmsford, N.Y.: Row, Peterson, 1962), pp. 91–92.

57. *Letters Home* has attracted few readers and fewer critics, but there are appreciative discussions in Oscar W. Firkins, *William Dean Howells* (Cambridge: Harvard University Press, 1922), and George N. Bennett, *The Realism of William Dean Howells, 1889–1920* (Nashville: Vanderbilt University Press, 1973). Van Wyck Brooks, who lists *Letters Home* among Howells's best dozen novels, quotes William James's ecstatic reaction: "You've done it this time and no mistake. I've just read *Letters Home,* which raised me from the dead almost, and which is the most absolutely faultless piece of richness as well as veracity that ever flowed out of human pen. I bar no one and no language. It is nature itself, and the wit of it, and the humour of it and the goodness of it! You may go—*that* will remain"; see *Howells: His Life and World* (New York: Dutton, 1959), pp. 286, 195–96 n.

58. Hired during the reorganization of Harper and Brothers, Frederick A. Duneka was a former colleague of Colonel Harvey on the *New York World.* He served as a general manager for the house and also as secretary to the board of directors. Duneka, who also worked with Mark Twain and Booth Tarkington, became Howells' editor after 1900. He was "an able executive, made decisions promptly, and was especially considerate of the older employees, from Alden down"; see Eugene Exman, *The House of Harper: One Hundred and Fifty Years of Publishing* (New York: Harper and Row, 1967), p. 188. Like Harvey, Duneka was younger than Howells and far more attuned to the increasingly commercial ethos of publishing.

59. Early in 1910, as Elinor's terminal illness and its associated costs escalated, Howells asked for a raise from $10,000 to $12,000 a year, to which the publishers readily agreed.

60. Cady, *The Realist at War,* p. 252. Howells's unsought appointment as the Academician, Cady proposes, may be dated from 1904, the year of his Oxford degree as well as the year he became a charter member of the American Academy of Arts and Letters. If there is to be any useful distinction between The Dean and the Academician—with the Academician understood to be an attenuation of The Dean—then it makes better sense to place Howells's transition from one role to the other in 1912, on the occasion of his seventy-fifth birthday party. From this event until his death eight years later, he became more and more a shadow of himself even as, paradoxically, he became more and more substantial a target for his enemies.

61. J. Henry Harper, *The House of Harper: A Century of Publishing in Franklin Square* (New York: Harper, 1912), pp. 319, 325–26. Although Howells' dictated recollections were intended for Harper's use as background, the publisher found the piece so charming that he included it complete in his book. It also appeared separately, soon after Howells's seventy-fifth birthday dinner, in the *New York Evening Post.* This slightly abbreviated version of the text is reprinted as "Mr. Howells's Paper" in *Criticism and Fiction and Other Essays,* ed. Clara Marburg Kirk and Rudolf Kirk (New York: New York University Press, 1959), pp. 377–84.

62. Arthur Gilman, "Atlantic Dinners and Diners," *Atlantic Monthly* 100 (November 1907): 647, 651.

63. While he was dictating his *Autobiography* in January 1906, Clemens picked up the

newfangled telephone to reach Howells, who incredulously told his brother: "Mark Twain called me up by his secretary today—she is a very gentle young girl,—and had her ask me over the 'phone 'what occasion it was in Boston when he *raised hell*' about Emerson and Longfellow" (*SL,* 5:157).

64. Exman, *The House of Harper,* p. 189.

65. *Life in Letters,* 2:313.

66. One sign of carefully coordinated public relations is an interview with Howells that was planted in the *New York Times* just before the birthday party. The interviewer, Henry Rood, who was an editor at *Harper's Monthly,* asserted that the dinner "will rank with four like celebrations which American literary history records—to name them chronologically, those in honor of Longfellow, Stoddard, Clemens, and Alden" (*Interviews,* pp. 96–97).

67. A published report put the number of tables at fifty. It seems likely that Howells was exaggerating.

68. Quoted in *Life in Letters,* 2:315.

69. Details about the 1912 affair and quotations from the speeches are taken from "The 75th Birthday Dinner: In Honor of Mr. Howells," a supplement to *Harper's Weekly* 56 (9 March 1912); repr. in *Critical Essays on W. D. Howells,* pp. 218–30.

70. See *Critical Essays on W. D. Howells,* pp. 215–18.

71. "Mr. Howells's Speech," *North American Review* 195 (April 1912); repr. in *Criticism and Fiction and Other Essays,* pp. 366, 368.

72. Harper, *The House of Harper,* p. 323. Howells also lashed out here at "the wild efflorescence of the historic novel, written so largely by people who knew so little history and read by people who knew it possibly less" (pp. 323–24).

73. "Mr. Howells's Speech," pp. 369–70, 372.

74. Heinz Ickstadt, "Howells' Idea of the Reading Public," *Revue Française D'Etudes Américaines* 8 (May 1983): 258. To Henry F. May, the Howells dinner "was really a testimonial to the unity, excellence, and continuity of American nineteenth-century civilization"—a traditional set of doctrines governing American art, business, and politics. Although these doctrines were "unquestioned by most of the diners at Sherry's and most other articulate Americans" in 1912, they were "already under attack in a few quarters and would soon be publicly torn apart"; see *The End of American Innocence: A Study of the First Years of Our Own Time, 1912–1917* (New York: Knopf, 1959), pp. 6, 8.

75. Michael Anesko, *Letters, Fictions, Lives: Henry James and William Dean Howells* (New York: Oxford University Press, 1997), pp. 455–56.

76. F. Scott Fitzgerald, *The Crack-Up,* ed. Edmund Wilson (New York: New Directions, 1945), p. 75.

77. Four months later, perhaps still enchanted by the "divine madness" of the ordeal, Howells wrote to Elizabeth Jordan, editor of *Harper's Bazar,* about something he had "madly imagined" giving her: "a series of social studies in the form of Twelve Distinctive Dinners, through which I should carry the hero and heroine in the character of observers or witnesses." Their adventures in the gustatory picaresque would range from "the first simple homelike meal of their childhood at noon to some final half-past eight o'clock

gorge in the highest life possible"; that is, from the simple family suppers of Howells's own childhood to the glutting and guzzling at Sherry's sixty years later. But Howells found he could not write this story: "I have not the nerve for it now, and may never have" (*SL*, 6:20).

78. Lewis P. Simpson, "The Treason of William Dean Howells," in *The Man of Letters in New England and the South: Essays on the History of the Literary Vocation in America* (Baton Rouge: Louisiana State University Press, 1973), pp. 90–91.

79. *Life in Letters*, 2:313.

80. Ibid., 2:322.

5. A DEAD CULT

1. The idea of a "posthumous" existence had arisen for Howells as early as his seventieth birthday in 1907, the same year in which Henry Adams issued the private edition of his *Education* and became as if "dead" among the living. "They made something of an ado over my birthday in the papers," Howells wrote to his brother, "and I thought some of the poor fellows in their kindness to me, had robbed their standing obituary notices. However, if I live long enough, people will forget that they read something like it before" (*SL*, 5:216).

2. Henry James, "A Letter to Mr. Howells" (1912), in *Critical Essays on W. D. Howells, 1866–1920*, ed. Edwin H. Cady and Norma W. Cady (Boston: G. K. Hall, 1983), p. 233.

3. Edwin H. Cady, *The Realist at War: The Mature Years, 1885–1920, of William Dean Howells* (Syracuse: Syracuse University Press, 1958), p. 255. Other quotations are identified in the text.

4. The same image, with a very different spin, was used by J. Henry Harper in 1912 to praise Howells' achievements: "Mr. Howells, who has so worthily earned his title of 'Dean of American Letters,' is a literary diamond of so many brilliant facets that it would be idle for me to attempt the slightest explication of his genius in the space or with the talents at my disposal"; see *The House of Harper: A Century of Publishing in Franklin Square* (New York: Harper, 1912), p. 318.

5. Gertrude Atherton, "Why Is American Literature Bourgeois?" (1904), in *The War of the Critics Over William Dean Howells*, ed. Edwin H. Cady and David L. Frazier (Evanston, Ill. and Elmsford, N.Y.: Row, Peterson, 1962), pp. 100, 102.

6. Frank Norris, "A Plea for Romantic Fiction," in *The Responsibilities of the Novelist* (1903; repr. New York: Hill and Wang, 1967), p. 280. As a dreadfully perfect specimen of what Norris and Atherton meant by the stultifying effects of Howellsian realism, consider Mary Arnold Childs's "William D. Howells: A Sonnet—After Reading His New Book, 'Miss Bellard's Inspiration' ":

> Let other greatness revel in displays
> Of tragic incident and passions wild;
> Thy greatness is enamoured of life's mild,

Tame, average and ordinary phase;
The dull routine of uneventful days
Thy keen imagination has beguiled
To chronicles of fiction undefiled,
Thou necromancer of the commonplace!

Whoe'er for stronger heroine forsook
The pleasing "Lady of the Aroostook,"
His lawless fancy never can have known
Thy placid realism's subtle thrill.
O! poet soul who didst the harp disown,
Thy fame is reckoned with the harpers, still.

This poem is so quintessentially expressive of "Littleism" that one only wishes it could confidently be read as a parody. (Its source is unknown to me; I found it glued to the rear pastedown of a first edition of *The World of Chance* [1893]).

7. *The War of the Critics,* p. 101.

8. *The Journal of Arthur Stirling* (New York: Appleton, 1903), pp. 159–60. This novel, published anonymously by Sinclair, was mistaken by some reviewers for a real journal. In a tribute after Howells's death, the publisher Henry Holt shrewdly speculated: "We are really inclined to believe that his denial of genius to anybody was due to a reluctance to admit that one man should naturally be so far endowed above other men, and, especially, to claim such endowment for himself. This state of mind goes far to explain why he tried to pull the great authors from their pedestals, as well as the great capitalists from their vantage points." At a dinner one evening Holt overheard Howells declaiming to Augustus Saint-Gaudens that there was no such thing as genius, to which the sculptor replied: "What do you call it when you see it?" See *Garrulities of an Octogenarian Editor* (Boston: Houghton Mifflin, 1923), p. 246.

9. *Martin Eden* (1909); repr. in *Jack London: Novels and Social Writings,* ed. Donald Pizer (New York: Library of America, 1982), p. 738. Burgess is usually credited with the coinage of the word "bromide," to mean something or someone soporifically dull.

10. *The War of the Critics,* p. 102.

11. *The Literary Guillotine* (New York and London: John Lane, 1903), p. 34. Other quotations are identified in the text. Although the editors of *Selected Letters* identify the author of this anonymously published book as Oliver Herford (*SL,* 5:111 n), the *National Union Catalogue* attributes it instead to William Wallace Whitelock.

12. Although the James and Fuller novels under review (*The Soft Side* and *The Last Refuge*) were issued, respectively, by Macmillan and Houghton Mifflin, both authors had earlier published with Harper and Brothers and thus were still affiliated with Franklin Square insofar as the fortunes of their current and future books would affect the sales of those on the Harper backlist.

13. William Lyon Phelps, *Essays on Modern Novelists* (New York: Macmillan, 1910),

pp. 59–60, 64–65. Phelps was responding to "Gertrude Atherton Assails 'The Powers,'" *New York Times,* 29 December 1907, later reprinted as "Why Have We Not More Great Novelists?" *Current Literature* 44 (February 1908): 158–60.

14. Alfred Bendixen, introduction to *The Whole Family: A Novel by Twelve Authors* (1908; repr. New York: Ungar, 1986), p. xiii. Throughout my discussion I draw from Bendixen's superb account of "The Whole Story Behind *The Whole Family.*" (Hereafter referred to as *WF.*)

15. The idea of collectively written fiction dates from the nineteenth century. Cynthia Ozick points to the game of "Rigmarole" in *Little Women* (1868), where "one person starts a story, a sentence or two, and the next person continues it." In *Roughing It* (1872), Mark Twain recalled a newspaper in Virginia City whose enterprising staff had hoped to boost circulation by writing a serial novel together. That same year Harriet Beecher Stowe, Edward Everett Hale, and four others collaborated on *Six of One by Half a Dozen of the Other* (1872). The immediate precedent for *The Whole Family* was *A House Party* (1901), to which a dozen notable writers, including Sarah Orne Jewett, George Washington Cable, and Owen Wister, anonymously contributed stories to a loosely bound narrative, leaving it to readers to guess their identities for a thousand-dollar prize. In recent days the idea has been revived virtually: John Updike "has lent his name, and his words, to an online collaborative writing contest in which Web surfers contribute a few lines each to a mystery story with an opening paragraph written by Updike" (AP story in the *Syracuse Post-Standard,* 14 August 1997; this story is also the source of the quotation from Ozick).

16. Bendixen believes, despite Jordan's assertions the contrary, "that James was one of the last authors to join *The Whole Family* and that he was actually a replacement for [Henry Blake] Fuller who apparently dropped out" (*WF,* xliii). Mark Twain was also among those who declined a bid to join *The Whole Family;* he later crowed that he had sensed a disaster in the offing.

17. Elizabeth Jordan, *Three Rousing Cheers* (New York: Appleton, 1938), pp. 273, 269, 272.

18. For a development of this point within a broader discussion of *The Whole Family,* see my review-essay: "The Whole Famdamnily," *New England Quarterly* 60 (March 1987): 106–13.

19. Jordan, *Three Rousing Cheers,* pp. 263–64.

20. Ibid., pp. 266–67, 264, 267.

21. Ibid., pp. 263, 267.

22. Cady, *The Realist at War,* pp. 256–57.

23. Alexander Harvey, *William Dean Howells: A Study of the Achievement of a Literary Artist* (New York: Huebsch, 1917), pp. 16, 27. The first doctoral dissertation on Howells, by Delmar Gross Cooke, also dates from 1917. Written at the University of Illinois, Cooke's thesis was eventually published as *William Dean Howells: A Critical Study* (New York: Dutton, 1922),

24. *Book Review Digest, 1917* (New York: H. W. Wilson, 1918), p. 252. All other quotations from the reviews of Harvey's book are taken from the same source.

25. This passage is quoted from the index entry under "Howells, William Dean," where Harvey placed what might have been the preface of a more conventional book.

Here he offers a thumbnail sketch of Howells's career and suggests that some day he may write a full-scale biography. Fortunately for Howells, Harvey's interest dissipated, but he did produce an introduction for the Modern Library edition of *A Hazard of New Fortunes* (New York: Boni and Liveright, 1917).

26. Not coincidentally, the publisher of *William Dean Howells,* B. W. Huebsch, also published *Winesburg, Ohio* (1919) and Anderson's other early books. Harvey's study might be seen as the critical counterpart to Anderson's baroque Freudian fantasia, *Many Marriages* (1923). As the American publisher also of James Joyce and D. H. Lawrence, as well as of André Tridon's *Psychoanalysis: Its History, Theory, and Practice* (1919), an early American primer, Huebsch was closely identified during the early 1920s with popular Freudianism and its radical promise of sexual liberation.

27. John A. Macy, *The Spirit of American Literature* (1913; repr. New York: Boni and Liveright, 1923), pp. 288–89. A confirmatory counterexample is Harriet Waters Preston's review of *The Kentons,* where what aroused her hostility was not the presence of Howells's "femininity," but the *absence* of his usual feline charm: "His playful wit, so whimsical and yet so natural, hiding often under a mask of gentle irony the quiver of an all but unmanageable tenderness, his gift of cunning observation, his tone, at once candid and demure, his honest, if queer convictions, and deep illogical earnestness,—all these things contribute to a mental make-up, a little more feminine than masculine perhaps, but very distinguished, and irresistibly attractive; see "The Latest Novels of Howells and James" (1903); in *The War of the Critics,* p. 91.

28. Henry Mills Alden, *Magazine Writing and The New Literature* (New York: Harper, 1908), p. 64.

29. H. L. Mencken, "The Dean" (1917, 1919), in *Critical Essays on W. D. Howells,* pp. 259–62.

30. *Critical Essays on W. D. Howells,* p. xxix.; *The Realist at War,* p. 258.

31. Van Wyck Brooks, *Opinions of Oliver Allston* (New York: Dutton, 1941), p. 22. This encounter was also recalled in *Van Wyck Brooks: An Autobiography* (New York: Dutton, 1965), p. 131.

32. "The Counsel of Literary Age to Literary Youth" (1904), in *Imaginary Interviews* (New York: Harper, 1910), pp. 283, 285.

33. Quoted in William Wasserstrom, *The Legacy of Van Wyck Brooks: A Study of Maladies and Motives* (Carbondale: Southern Illinois University Press, 1971), p. 17.

34. Brooks, *An Autobiography,* pp. 157, 270. Brooks, whose last book would be *Howells: His Life and World* (New York: Dutton, 1959), came to embrace him warmly; "for, in spite of his conventional entanglements, Howells had a beautiful feeling for life and a spacious and generous understanding of it." Brooks recalled that after their meeting in 1909, Howells had spontaneously invited the interviewer to ride along with him on one of the new Fifth Avenue motorbuses: "and I remember the alert curiosity with which, from our seat on the top, this old story-teller studied the crowds on the sidewalks" (pp. 157–58).

35. "Mr. Howells at Work at Seventy-Two" (1909), in *Interviews with William Dean Howells,* ed. Ulrich Halfmann (Arlington, Tex.: American Literary Realism, 1973), p. 88. Other quotations are identified in the text.

36. Brooks confessed in 1941: "Allston never forgot Howells's good sense and kindness, although many years passed before he read Howells's novels. He was forty-five before he knew how good they were" (*Opinions of Oliver Allston*, pp. 22–23). Later he wrote that "this hero of the young realistic novelists was naturally annoyed that I had not read more of his own novels. I doubt if I had read more than one, though I was to read them all in time" (*An Autobiography*, p. 157). In the 1909 interview, Brooks refers to *The World of Chance* in an informed way that suggests he must, in fact, have read it. It somehow seems fitting that the one Howells novel Brooks really knew was the one about an ambitious young man coming to New York in quest of literary fame and fortune.

37. James R. Vitelli, introduction to Van Wyck Brooks, *Three Essays on America* (New York: Dutton, 1970), p. xx.

38. Ibid., p. 139.

39. Van Wyck Brooks, *The Ordeal of Mark Twain* (New York: Dutton, 1920), pp. 68–69.

40. Although it was assumed by his contemporaries that Brooks had read deeply in Freud, it seems that his firsthand knowledge of psychoanalysis was as shallow as his familiarity with Howells' writings. (In neither case, however, did ignorance deter Brooks from affecting erudition.) William Wasserstrom, pursuing a tip from Robert E. Spiller, has traced Brooks's "pioneering studies in literary psychology" to a single source: Bernard Hart, *The Psychology of Insanity* (1912), which assimilated certain Freudian notions (the unconscious and the idea of repression) into a crude method "of discovering simple trauma behind complicated events." According to Spiller, Brooks once admitted to him that "Hart's little book represented all that he knew of psychoanalysis. Whether or not he read Freud or Jung too, whom he mentions in print now and then, is uncertain." "Van Wyck Brooks," in *Van Wyck Brooks: The Critic and His Critics*, ed. William Wasserstrom (Port Washington, N.Y.: Kennikat, 1979), p. 215.

41. Régis Michaud, *The American Novel To-Day: A Social and Psychological Study* (Boston: Little, Brown, 1928), pp. 67–68.

42. Sinclair Lewis, "The American Fear of Literature" (1930), in *The Man from Main Street: Selected Essays and Other Writings, 1904–1950*, ed. Harry E. Maule and Melville H. Cane (New York: Random House, 1953), pp. 15–16.

43. Fred Lewis Pattee, *Tradition and Jazz* (New York: Century, 1925), pp. 112–13.

44. The manifesto, as it were, of the "Howells revival" was Kenneth E. Eble's anthology, *Howells: A Century of Criticism* (Dallas, Tex.: Southern Methodist University Press, 1962). The term itself apparently was coined by James Woodress in "The Dean's Comeback: Four Decades of Howells Scholarship" (1960): "During the past two decades the Howells revival has snowballed. In every type of activity from doctoral dissertation to book-length study Howells has been measured and analyzed by a steadily growing number of scholars" (*Howells: A Century of Criticism*, p. 238). Although several fine young scholars did decide during this period to dedicate their careers, at least in part, to the pursuit of Howellsian research, the snowball soon stopped rolling and then began to melt: the number of such scholars was steadily diminishing by the last quarter of the century.

45. Edwin Harrison Cady, "A Note on Howells and 'The Smiling Aspects of Life,'" *American Literature* 17 (May 1945): 175–78; repr. in Eble, ed., *Howells: A Century of Criticism,* p. 159.

46. Part of that formulation, as we have seen, derived from psychoanalysis; although Cady's summary of the anti-Howellsian line makes no explicit reference to its specifically Freudian aspect, he implicitly adduces the "Oedipus Complex" to explain the younger generation's "natural" antagonism. In effect, Cady's anti-anti-Howellsian tactics turned psychoanalysis against itself, outpsyching such Freudians as Brooks by exposing the unconsciously rivalrous aggression that motived their misapprehension of Howells.

INDEX